PRACTICAL HORSEMANSHIP
IN
SHOW AND FIELD

John Board's

PRACTICAL HORSEMANSHIP
IN
SHOW AND FIELD

By

HUGH VENABLES M.R.C.V.S.

With the original line drawings by Major John Board

(Cover photograph by Bob Langrish)

PAPERFRONTS

ELLIOT RIGHT WAY BOOKS
KINGSWOOD, SURREY, U.K.

CONTENTS

Making friends

INTRODUCTION

Art may be one and indivisible, but each branch of it has its own individual technique: painting, music, literature, drama. The same can be said of the Equestrian Art.

Though its principles are constant, each branch is specialised and calls for differing methods on the part of the rider, as it does for differing qualities in the horse. For all aspects of equitation, however, there are certain essentials. For the rider, whether proposing simply to hack in the parks and along the country lanes, or having ambitions to become a fox-hunter, horse trials competitor, show jumper or dressage expert, or all of these together, it is a prime necessity to know and understand the horse, the vehicle of our pleasure.

The rider must also be able to help the horse to give of his best performance and thus provide the utmost pleasure. It is true that no active pursuit can be learned from the written word alone. It is only by practical experience that we can be taught. But the written word has its uses in forming a mental background on which the practical art can be developed, and in providing a useful reference in our various perplexities. And for most people who enjoy being with horses, reading about them and their training is also a source of pleasure.

The greatest charm of what is generally known as equitation (and this includes the essential knowledge of how to keep a horse fit and well) is that, even though one may spend a lifetime on and with horses and among riders, one never stops learning. The absolutely perfect rider, like the absolutely perfect horse, has yet to be seen. One of the reasons is that, just as no two people are alike, so also are no two horses alike, temperamentally or physically, so that the rider must subtly adjust to each individual mount in order to get the best out of it.

To do this demands knowledge, experience, practice and understanding. But there are many riders who approach perfection and are a joy to watch in action, and also many who can be described as thoroughly efficient. Even for them, however, there is always something new to be learned and stored away for possible future use, so that there is never any finality. The charm of the novel, the unexpected, is with us always.

There are some who possess an instinct and sympathy for horses which appears to amount to genius. Such people are enviable, and to be admired and imitated. But most of their skill is the result of careful and sensitive study of the animal, often unconscious, which allows them to anticipate a horse's reactions under any circumstances. It also enables them to decide correctly which is the appropriate moment to make some demand of the animal, whether it is that he should stand still to have his feet picked out, or walk past an object of which he is genuinely terrified.

Much of this knowledge boils down to a feeling for the equine character. The horse is naturally a grazing beast, and has evolved as a herd animal which must be sensitive and responsive to the presence of many enemies. His immediate defence would be to run, the rest of the herd with him, far and fast, and away from danger. So it is not surprising that to be restrained in circumstances which are unfamiliar, and therefore frightening, can drive a horse to a state of wild and completely unreasoning panic. He has acute senses of smell and hearing, and sight which allows him to detect movement very readily although he may not be able to visualise things as accurately as we can. Sudden movements frighten him and it takes some time for his confidence to be restored.

Although he is sensitive he is of limited intelligence. He is dextrous when it comes to keeping his feet and leaping over obstacles, but this is not the same thing. He has no logical ability, although he can develop habits very easily, and the more precise the stimulus and the greater and more pleasing the reward, the quicker he will learn. If you bear this in mind in your dealings with horses and try to find an explanation for the animal's actions (there always is a sensible reason and it is very seldom plain awkwardness), you too will develop that envied 'feeling' for horses.

To become a competent equestrian is not beyond the capacity of anyone who really wants to do so and is prepared to work hard to attain this desire. Competence with horses is not an occult mystery as some would have us believe, but the 'we know—you don't and never will' faction exists in every sphere. Indeed, one of the most interesting developments in recent years, and to some of us among the most pleasing to witness, has been the establishment of riding and driving horses and ponies as a sport for the disabled. It has been found that for children and young adults who are very severely handicapped, physically or mentally, the sensation of riding on or driving a horse provides enormous pleasure and is also of great therapeutic value to those who may have no hope of ever walking unaided. It is not hard to imagine what a delight this must be when one thinks of the pleasure that a normal person derives from riding. Incidentally, riding for the disabled is provided primarily by the charity, in the form of money and physical assistance, of the riding public.

Let us take heart, therefore, sure in the knowledge that we can succeed if only we take the trouble to do so. But consider now a brief, but true, story. Not so long ago at a holiday resort two girls were discussing how they would spend the next day. One was asked whether she and her friend were going to ride again. 'Oh, no,' she answered, 'we learned that yesterday; tomorrow we're going to learn how to sail.' Certainly there are many beginners who fail to realise what they are letting themselves in for when they embark on a course of riding lessons. Were they do do so it is possible that many might hesitate at the prospect of a protracted period of elementary teaching, with all its pains and disappointments. But, on the other hand, these must be weighed against the novice rider's being able to measure, even from the very start, a concrete advance day by day, and enthusiasm is whetted by the promise of an equal or greater improvement tomorrow.

More and more people, from all walks of life, are turn-ing to horses as a means of escape and of obtaining the interest and exercise that they require. And what a wide range of activities are offered! A very little knowledge and experience will allow anyone to enjoy a weekly hack in the park or among the glorious country of the South Downs, the Wiltshire Plains, the hills of the West Country or of Scotland or Wales where great pleasure can also be obtained from pony trekking. For those who are more ambitious there lies a wide range of choices between the hunting field, where hounds may be seen at work and the countryside enjoyed to the full; the excitement of mounted games, from the high handicap polo match (which very few of us can even consider because of its cost) to less demanding games, such as paddock polo and cushion polo, and the gymkhana races, all of which are fostered by the Pony Club, which grows in strength from year to year; the hard competition in the show ring, whether showing horses and ponies in hand or under saddle, and the delights of training a horse and competing in horse trials or dressage competitions. Dressage is of particular interest because it is the basis for the training of any riding horse, and for the training of any horse rider.

In some equestrian pursuits, such as hunting and mounted games, the horse is a necessary adjunct, but one cannot devote one's entire attention to riding. In com-bined training, dressage, showing and show jumping the accent is more obviously on the riding. Anyone who wishes can learn enough to become a beginner at any of these delightful pastimes within a reasonably short time. But the rider can only become expert by steady applica-tion and the accumulation of experience until reactions are automatic and accurate; until, like Kipling's *The Nurses:*

'These have so utterly mastered their work that they work without thinking;
Holding three-fifths of their brain in reserve for what-ever betides.
And when catastrophe threatens, of colic, collision or sinking,

They shunt the full gear into train, and take the small thing in their stride.'

In the pages that follow an attempt has been made to clarify the essential differences in the various forms of equestrian endeavour, and their similarities, combined with observations based for the most part on personal experience. The rider whom it is intended that this book should help is the one who has emerged from the 'nursery' stage and now proposes to venture a little farther into the process of initiation into the noble art of equitation. Consequently, there is no need to discuss such elementary details as how to mount and dismount, to hold the reins or to apply the basic aids for these will have been mastered earlier in the novitiate's career.

The book has been based on 'Horses and Horsemen' which was published by the late Major John Board some years ago. Although equestrian sports have changed no less rapidly than the rest of the world during the intervening years, John Board was evidently well aware that this movement was in train, and that it was accelerating. Much of what he wrote in the early fifties is as true now as it was then. And of course in the years since, it is to be expected that some of the theses which were accepted then would be disproved or cease to be applicable, and these sections have been removed in Hugh Venables's up-dating of the new edition. But John Board's sensitive observations have provided a very interesting background and an unusual degree of insight into the development of riding as a sport which will, it is hoped, help the aspiring rider to get the several sections of the equestrian world into perspective.

As well as being an expert horseman, John Board was also a very considerable artist and his delightful sketches are retained in this edition. They also remind us of the radical differences in some aspects of the horse worlds of now and of a quarter of a century ago. Most noticeable is perhaps the complete acceptance of women in riding today, when a woman is unquestionably any man's equal and quite capable of taking him on—and beating him— on equal terms. Compare this with the novelty of having a Ladies' show jumping competition at the Olympia horse show in the early fifties.

Much has changed over those years, but these are certain constant principles in all forms of equitation, and have been for centuries. The chief essentials are enthusiasm, and a love and understanding for that simple yet complex ally, the horse. You also need to acquire a firm, independent, seat on top of him, for without this that subtle communion of interests, commonly known as 'hands', and full control, are both unattainable. The right way is, in the long run, the best way, though it may take a little longer to learn. But the reward is utterly beyond so small a drawback, and it always has been, and it always will be. It is the ability to enjoy in full partnership with the loveliest animal on earth the innumerable ecstasies which make up what we know as 'RIDING'.

I

ELEMENTARY EQUITATION

Temperament and Mechanics
The law very properly insists that nobody shall be allowed to drive a motor car on the public highway until he or she is capable of controlling the vehicle and is no longer likely to be a danger to other road users. Few of these people will be riders and in a mechanical age it is natural that the vast majority of motorists should have little experience of the horse or understanding of his natural reactions. Many people, through ignorance for the most part, fail to show reasonable consideration for the horse on the road. Consequently, one has to look out for oneself and ensure that a reasonable degree of skill and some experience has been accumulated before taking a horse on the public highway, or a serious accident may ensue.

At best, it is going to be very uncomfortable for the rider who tries to venture into public before attaining complete control of the horse. And when we begin to try our hand in the show ring or the hunting field this need is even greater, for now we are 'on our own'. Other riders have urgent business to attend to and little time to help the inexperienced rider who is in difficulties. And apart from their personal peril, inexperienced riders who are not in full control of their mounts are, at worst, a serious danger and, at best, a nuisance to other equestrians. But a few months' training in the riding 'school' should give the beginner sufficient confidence and skill to go out alone, which is when you will really begin to learn to ride.

Apart from the obvious need to remain on top of your horse and to know how to indicate your wishes to him, an understanding of his nature, best obtained in the stable, is the most important of all. Naturally, all of us would prefer to own our own horses, but that must come later and, unfortunately, is not always possible. But familiarity with the nature of the animal can be gained in other ways, such as frequent visits to the riding stable or to the stables of your friends' horses. Sociable creatures and liable to acute boredom in loneliness, horses appreciate attention, especially if it is augmented by an occasional titbit of carrot, bread or apple. Like his master, the way to the equine's heart is through his stomach. It is every bit as important to know how to look after him, clean him, and feed him, as it is to be able to sit on him. Until you can do all this, and maintain your own saddlery and equipment as well, you cannot claim to have mastered the art of equitation.

Far more people are nervous of horses than will ever admit it, and the surest cure for this is to spend a lot of time with them, handling them in their stables or turned out in their fields. The horse is a gentle animal, willing and able to give you great enjoyment, but he is of distinctly limited intelligence. The best way to treat him is as a backward child of five. He can only be trained by reward and punishment, plenty of the first and little, but sharp and firm, of the second. On the other hand, he is always anxious to please you, if only he can understand what you want.

Until you are secure in your seat and fully able to communicate your desires, with the means of enforcing them, like ninety nine out of a hundred novices you will experience moments of alarm, even panic. This will communicate itself instantly to any horse, who will react immediately to what he interprets as a warning of danger ahead. A full understanding of the equine temperament is therefore essential. Without it, and the sympathy that accompanies it, no rider, however competent in the purely physical aspect of riding, can hope to become an accomplished horseman.

Of almost equal importance is an at least superficial knowledge of the structure of the horse and of obvious symptoms of ill-health. If your car breaks down there is

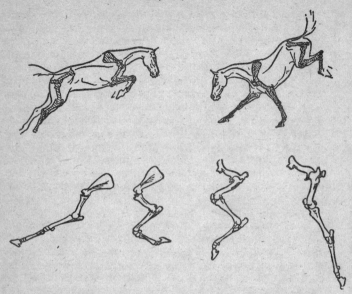

Action of joints. Fore and hind legs

nearly always another motorist on the road who will come to your aid. Out riding, the chances are that you will be thrown on your own resources. Problems of accident and equine illness are dealt with in a later chapter, but the anatomy of the horse, so far as it concerns locomotion, must be described briefly here and now, for without it the traditional art of equitation would be incomplete.

To some extent the horse may be likened to a traditional motor car. For instance, the energy that drives him forward is at the back, as the drive of a car is from the back axle. The impulse is given to the car by the combined actions of the driver's foot on the accelerator pedal and hand on the gear lever. The same applies to the riders 'aids', for the act of the hand on the rein combined with the action of the leg throws the horse into gear and provides the acceleration.

Motor cars are fitted with springs and shock absorbers. So are horses, with the compensating joints and ligaments of the limbs activated by the muscles and tendons which also support them. The hind-quarters of the animal provide the forward impulse and they are therefore constructed primarily to thrust backwards, while the primary function of the fore-quarters is to support the weight and reach forward as the animal moves along. A weak part of the structure is the area over that section of the spine between the last rib and the massive structure of the pelvis, and obviously the minimum of strain must be put on this part, which is called the loins. The rider does better to ensure that weight is put on the stronger point where the spine curves down towards the chest, just behind the shoulder.

The analogy between horse and car fails in some degree when it comes to steering. Though the hands, acting on the bit through the reins, do serve to change the direction of the head and so, to some extent, the direction of the body too, a horse can only be steered efficiently by a combination of leg and hand, with the accent on leg rather than hand. It is indeed possible to direct a well-trained horse by leg alone, though not by hand alone.

The head of the horse is very heavy, accounting for one-fifth of his entire weight, and he must use his whole body to control its position. Conversely, he cannot balance the rest of his body and perform efficiently if his head is not correctly placed. Control of the head and neck is given by the reins but once a horse has been taught to carry his head correctly he will make the necessary adjustments almost automatically. This balance is essential to both horse and rider and will only come to the horse through intelligent training and subsequent action by his rider, and to the rider only through the acquisition of a firm and independent seat.

Riding Schools
Today there are innumerable riding stables all over the country, nearly all of which will undertake elementary teaching. Provided you select those which are British Horse Society (BHS) Approved you may expect a good

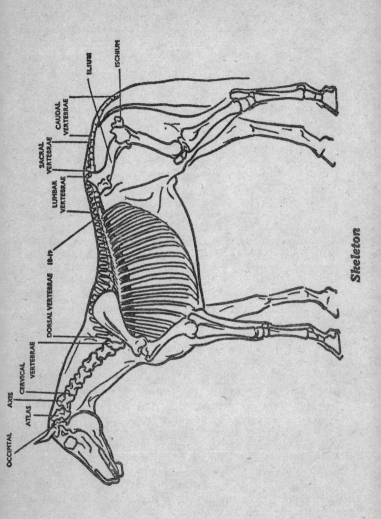

Skeleton

OCCIPITAL
ATLAS
AXIS
CERVICAL VERTEBRAE
DORSAL VERTEBRAE 18-19
LUMBAR VERTEBRAE
SACRAL VERTEBRAE
CAUDAL VERTEBRAE
ILIUM
ISCHIUM

Evolved from earlier styles

overall standard which is, in some cases, very high. Now
that regular inspection by a local authority-appointed
veterinary surgeon is required for all riding establishments, we see far fewer of those 'riding schools' which not
only fail to teach correct equitation but also fail to provide adequate stabling, feeding and care for the unfortunate, helpless animals which earn a living for them.
To learn to ride, and subsequently to enjoy all the
pleasures available to the rider, it is most important to
start right and to make certain that one is obtaining the
best possible value for money. Go, therefore, to an establishment of good repute whose instructors are well quali-
fied, by examination as well as experience; though you

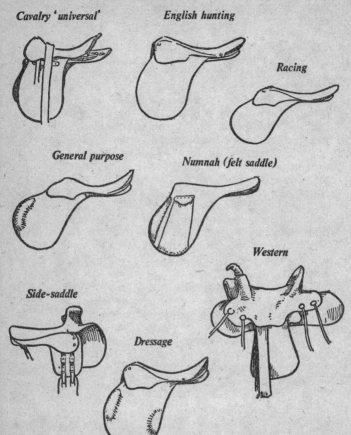

Cavalry 'universal'   English hunting

Racing

General purpose   Numnah (felt saddle)

Western

Side-saddle

Dressage

Various types of saddle

may have to travel farther and pay more, you will not regret it.

The saddle
The best saddle for the beginner is the modern 'general purpose' type which has evolved by trial and error from the earlier styles, such as the cavalry 'universal' which was designed for active service in the days when horse transport was still important in the European armies. Like the traditional English hunting saddles, it is rather too straight cut for the more modern style of riding which is suited better by the forward cut of the saddle flap and the 'central seat' of the general purpose saddle. The 'central seat' merely implies that, as one might logically expect, the lowest point of the seat of the saddle is in the middle, rather than pushed back, so that the rider is encouraged to sit in the right place. One of the greatest difficulties that the novice is likely to encounter is that of getting really *into* the saddle although to remember the old maxim 'sit up straight and tuck your tail in' is helpful.

Though the more obvious 'aids' are given by the hands and the lower leg, much impulse and control comes from higher up, by the transfer of weight on the part of the rider which is felt by the horse through the saddle. Incidentally, the expressions 'seat' and 'balance' are often misunderstood, which leads to many errors in equitation. 'Seat' suggests a position similar to that adopted when one sits down on a chair, when the outer part of the seat-bones, where the thigh-bone fits into its socket in the pelvis, is in contact with the chair's seat. That part of the seat-bones should be in only superficial contact with the saddle, the real, firm, contact being at the inner part of the joint. Until a rider can get this portion of the anatomy well into the central hollow of the saddle the position on a horse will be insecure and incorrect. Once a good seat in the saddle has been achieved it will be much easier for the rider to develop a stable, firm contact of inner thigh and knee with the saddle flap.

The word 'balance' suggests a precarious equilibrium maintained with great difficulty on an unstable or at least

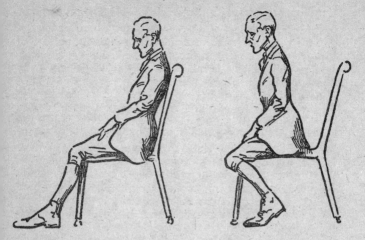

Resting in a chair, and adopting a 'seat' on it

a narrow base. The base, to be sure, is both unstable and narrow, but 'balance' as it is understood in equitation is far from unstable and depends to a considerable extent on a firm purchase on the base, for it is complementary to 'grip'.

There are those who will tell you that it is possible to ride effectively by balance alone, implying that grip is unnecessary. But do not believe them, for however well they may ride themselves, they do not really understand how they do it. Practice makes perfect and the practised rider certainly does not maintain a continuous, rigid, vice-like, grip on the saddle, but the grip is there and ready for application in response to the most sensitive of signals. A sloppy position in the saddle is an indication of ignorance and complacency just as much as a rigid one is a symptom of inexperience and uncertainty.

As the horse's head is the heaviest component of his body, so is that of the human frame. Accordingly, changes in its position, and of that of the upper part of the body, must be made to conform with the speed and change of direction of the horse. The faster the speed, the farther forward the head and torso, the more sudden the acceleration, as in a jump, the quicker and more violent the compensating change of the rider's position to give a combined fluency of action of horse and rider. This is known as 'going with the horse' and requires a firm, unshakeable, base from which to move. It is provided by the knee and inner part of the lower thigh when the seat is out of the saddle at fast paces and over fences, and by the whole length of the inner thigh when the seat is in the saddle. The farther down on the saddle flap the rider's knee can be forced, the more powerful the grip, the more secure the position and the more certain the balance.

To obtain a physical sensation of the meaning of 'getting into the saddle' first get the weight well forward into the hollow of the saddle and then allow the legs to drop to their fullest extent on either side. In this position the whole leg is relaxed so that very little power can be exercised. Next, lift the legs slightly so that the inner pad of the knee comes into direct contact with the saddle flap. This gives an immediate sense of power and security. Keeping the knees in position, next extend the heels downward to the fullest possible extent, at the same time forcing the sole of the foot slightly outwards. This will have the effect of drawing the foot a trifle to the rear so that the tip of the toe is in line with the front of the knee. Finally, adjust the stirrup leather until the iron can be slipped over the toe and checks immediately under the ball of the foot. If you can see more than the tips of your toes beyond the point of your knee when you look vertically downwards, they are too far forward, and if you have to crane forward to see them beyond your knee they are too far back.

As a rough and ready method of adjusting the stirrup leather before mounting, it will be found that with the knuckles on the bar by which the leathers are fastened to the saddle, the bottom of the stirrup iron should barely reach the armpit. Slight adjustments to suit the peculiarities of horse and human, and to match the type of

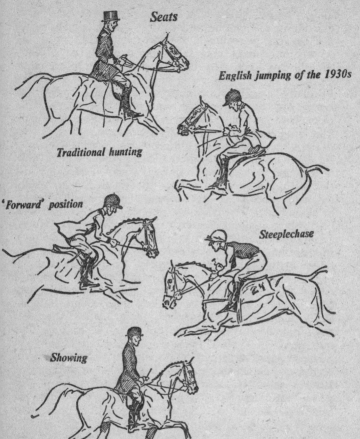

Seats

Traditional hunting

English jumping of the 1930s

'Forward' position

Steeplechase

Showing

riding, may subsequently be necessary, but this is a fairly safe rule to ensure that on arrival in 'the plate' you are at least reasonably secure and comfortable. This most elementary adjustment may seem over-stressed, but without it one is bound to start wrong and therefore to continue wrong.

Broadly speaking, the more violent the exercise, the shorter you will have to make your stirrup leathers.

For instance you will find that for hunting, in which your progress varies from a slow hound-jog to a full gallop, with jumps over natural objects of varying shapes and sizes on uneven surfaces, to the sudden halts and turns which are incidental all day, you will need to ride with stirrups one or two holes shorter than you would for steady hacking or for showing a horse on the flat in the show ring.

For show jumping, hunter trials and the cross country phase of combined training events you would need to ride shorter still, since you must keep your weight off the saddle so that it impedes as little as possible the horse's upward and forward impulsion as he leaps and gallops. You must still retain firm control, and the vertical line from point of knee to tip of toe should be maintained. The forward cut of the modern saddle flap and the padding or 'knee roll' at its front all help you to keep this position.

The greater the activity, the more you will need to free the horse's loins and shorten the stirrup leathers. But however short we ride, the position of the knee on the saddle flap remains constant until we come to flat racing, in which it is often clear above the saddle, the grip, what there is of it, being maintained by the lower part of the leg. This jockey style of riding came to Britain relatively recently, the celebrated jockeys of earlier times riding with their legs fully extended and their seats firmly in the saddle. Less dramatically and more recently the 'forward seat' which is generally adopted for general purpose riding nowadays arrived from the continental cavalry schools, and since the Second World War has gradually supplanted the traditional 'sitting down and leaning back'

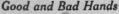

Good and Bad Hands

style of the English hunting field and the early show jumping competitions.

'Hands'

No two horses are the same and it is only by individual experiment that we can find the bit that suits a horse best. Nearly all equine misbehaviour is attributable either to over-excitement (just like a small child) or to some discomfort or pain which is often caused by ill-fitting harness or unsuitable bitting. Most horses start life with good mouths, but many are quickly deprived of this essential quality by heavy handling and early introduction to over-severe bits. Like a human's, a horse's mouth is a very sensitive part of his body and a heavy hand on the rein causes him acute pain. He has, too, an extremely vivid memory, particularly for experiences which were associated with pain or fear, and much intractability can be attributed to discomfort he has already suffered. A heavy hand is a direct result of an insecure seat, though it is occasionally noticeable in those who have reputations as 'strong' riders.

Really good hands are often thought to be a rare gift, but reasonably light hands can be developed by almost anyone who is willing to work to acquire a strong seat in the saddle, independent of the reins, and above all a sympathetic understanding of the horse as an animal with little logic, a strong herd instinct, and an innate tendency to panic when frightened.

Our teaching insists on a continual connection or 'contact' between the horse's mouth and the rider's hands by means of the reins; For European trained horses this is the basis for their training. But in the cattle countries of North America, Australia and Argentina, on the other hand, the cow ponies are trained to work on a slack rein with only an occasional contact between hand and mouth for an emergency halt. Changes of direction are indicated by the leg and shifting of the weight, with the pressure of a still slack rein against the horse's neck on the side from which it is desired that he shall turn.

Indeed, once a horse has been taught to carry his head properly, and so can balance himself, it is not difficult to teach him to obey western-style neck reining. It helps to make him a more responsive ride, and for mounted games, such as gymkhanas and polo, it is almost essential.

The need for a rider to be in full control of the horse whatever the circumstances has already been pointed out. This means being able to make the animal stand still to be mounted, and to stand still when the rider is aboard, too; to be able to walk, trot or canter as desired, and in collected, ordinary or extended fashion; to turn the horse on his haunches, centre or forehand; to rein back and to move sideways; to jump from a walk, trot or canter and to leave other horses and proceed in the desired direction without argument.

In the case of the schooled horse these are all easy, but all horses are not well schooled and the ones we hire are apt to have inconsistent reactions when we consider the different 'aids', intentional and unintentional, to which they are subjected by a legion of different riders in the course of any working day.

Bridles

The popular bit today is the jointed snaffle in its various forms, with plain rings, or with rings and cheeks attached to the bridle to hold the bit stable in the horse's mouth. In most instances it is the jointed snaffle which is used, although it must be remembered that, particularly if the mouthpiece is thin, the action of this bit is not on the bars of the mouth but more like a nutcracker, pinching the lips and sometimes bruising the cheeks and jaw bones.

A more gentle version of the snaffle is the straight or slightly curved (half moon) one, made of metal or rubber, and without the joint in the middle of the mouthpiece. Most horses will behave very well in this bit. Frequently used with a snaffle bit is the 'dropped' noseband, which is designed so that the front part of the horizontal strap lies well clear of the horse's nostrils while the back part buckles below the bit, under his chin. The object of this is not to prevent the unfortunate animal from opening his mouth but to ensure that the bit makes contact with sensitive corners of the mouth and for this reason the dropped noseband should not be tight.

A common error is the belief than an excitable or hard-mouthed animal will be held more easily with a mass of metal in his mouth and contraptions round his head than in a simple bridle. This fallacy is based on the erroneous idea that a human being can get the better in a trial of strength with an animal twenty times as strong. The harder you pull and the more pain you impose, the harder the horse will pull; the more the bit hurts him, the harder he will pull in a vain attempt to escape the pain. But he will not stop for it nor will be quieten down; rather he will 'hot up' more and more.

There is only one way to get a horse under control again when he takes off, as most horses will do from time to time through over-keenness and excitement. Rectify his balance by first getting his hocks under him again and by 'fixing' your hand to get his head up at the moment of suspension only, letting the contact between your hands and his mouth become light as his forehand comes to the ground.

Persistent give and take in this manner, applied gently

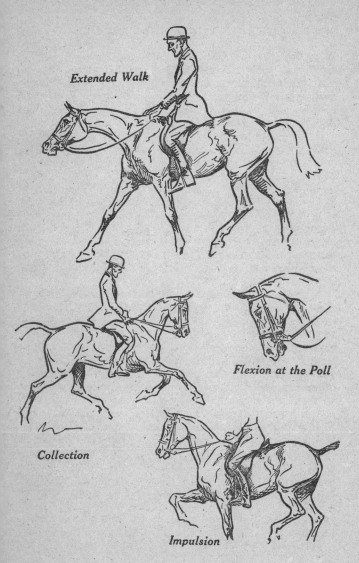

Extended Walk

Flexion at the Poll

Collection

Impulsion

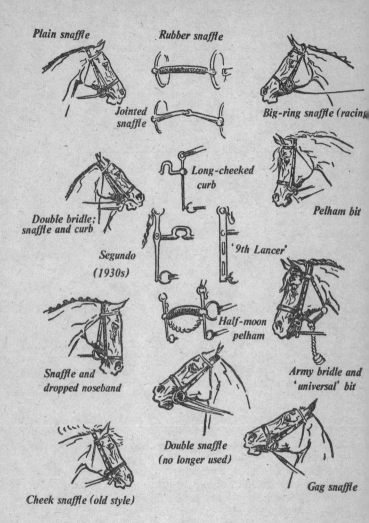

Plain snaffle

Rubber snaffle

Jointed snaffle

Big-ring snaffle (racing)

Long-cheeked curb

Double bridle; snaffle and curb

Pelham bit

Segundo (1930s)

'9th Lancer'

Half-moon pelham

Snaffle and dropped noseband

Army bridle and 'universal' bit

Cheek snaffle (old style)

Double snaffle (no longer used)

Gag snaffle

The harder he will pull

but firmly, will sooner or later restore your mastery of the situation. This, and the use of the voice in a soothing tone (never shout at a horse; he does not understand your threats and only becomes more frightened) will bring him back to hand.

The curb bit acts very differently from the snaffle, and may, as in the 'double' bridle be used as a complement to it. The curb nowadays almost invariably consists of a straight bar in the horse's mouth, and the rein attached to the bottom of the cheek activates a lever system which tightens and slackens the curb chain round his jaw. The curb bits which have been used for centuries on the mules and asses of Northern Africa are obviously designed to break the animals' jaws with the minimum of effort to the person in control, but in European riding the object of

B

Horse's head and neck overbent

the curb's lever action is to apply a very sensitive stimulus by the touch of the curb chain and the rotation of the bar of the bit in the horse's mouth. The action of the rein through the curb is more of a warning than a direct order, for the executive command will come through the thighs and lower leg.

The pressure on the bit helps to 'collect' the horse ready for a change of pace of direction.

To realise how the horse feels it is valuable to have taken part at some time in one's life in cross-country running, and also to have carried another person pick-a-back. In the latter you are acutely conscious that your centre of gravity or point of balance has shifted considerably. The horse feels exactly the same thing and so it is obviously desirable to minimise the difference as much as

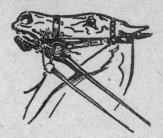

Needless suffering

you can by automatically adjusting your position in accordance with increases and decreases of pace and with changes in direction so that the effect of the inertia of your body is as small as possible.

Fear born of ignorance will make the unschooled horse offer a defence to every 'aid' given by the rider, that is, until he learns that to give the desired response is more rewarding. This is achieved only by patient repetition until he responds. Only in the last resort should punishment in the shape of pain be inflicted, though if you have to hit a horse do hit him hard with a 'one-two' on his ribs, behind the saddle flap, so that he is in no doubt about your feelings.

'An Awfully Big Adventure'

To the novice, jumping seems a tremendous and alarming adventure and, until one discovers for oneself how simple it is to go with a horse over a jump, one is apt to invest it with an importance and difficulty that it really does not warrant. For that reason the sooner the beginner goes over a small jump in the school the better for his confidence and progress. The secret is to keep the knees firmly in their correct place, to raise the seat-bones just clear of the saddle as the horse completes his final stride and then lean well forward, to counteract the sudden acceleration

An awfully big adventure

of the actual leap, and to free a horse's mouth so that he can stretch his neck right forward. No beginner should jump without a neckstrap as an aid to keeping forward and avoiding a jerk on the horse's mouth.

Nearly all horses enjoy jumping and for the rider it gives perhaps the greatest exhilaration of all. But in this, just as in all other gaits and movements, it is not enough to be able to remain on top. One must be able to help one's horse. More horses are made to refuse and to fall by a fault of the rider than ever do so of their own volition. How often have you seen a loose horse fall in a steeple-chase? Very, very, seldom, if ever, and then probably through putting his foot through a rein or being knocked by another. But a ridden horse will refuse a jump often enough. The chief cause is nearly always the rider's lack of determination to go over, or his interference which has either checked the horse just as he needed all the freedom he could be given, or by an error of timing which

A horse will refuse often enough

has resulted in the horse's being brought to his take-off point too close to the fence or too far from it for him to be able to clear it. An experienced horse can generally be depended upon to take good care of himself and his rider, but even he must be given a reasonable chance to do so.

Many horses are apt to rush their fences through excitement and this is a common cause of falls. Patient training, trotting over poles on the ground and working over cavaletti, small fences in series, will help to steady the animal and encourage him to take more care. Above all he must be convinced that the leap is not going to be accompanied by any pain or discomfort, for a large proportion of those animals which rush wildly at their fences do so as an alternative to refusing.

Training over trotting poles and cavaletti will also teach the rider to go with the horse's movements and to rely on knees and thighs to maintain a forward position, just out of the saddle and supple enough not to be thrown out of balance by the animal's more violent action as he jumps. Until you have learned to perform these basic movements with confidence you cannot be regarded as competent to go out on your own and certainly not to take on the more demanding challenges of hunter trials, combined training events and the show jumping ring.

Lastly, it is worth remembering that the ultimate impression of the finished rider is that the application of the aids is scarcely noticeable, the firm position being combined with a notable suppleness. This can only be acquired by practice.

2

HUNTING

Introduction

To its enthusiasts, hunting, and especially fox-hunting, is more than a sport. It is a National Institution, enjoyed equally by all countrymen, for in the hunting field social distinctions do not exist and those who follow hounds start equal, receiving consideration and attaining eminence exclusively through their own merits.

For very many years the local hunt has been closely associated with the life of the countryside and indeed its functions still are as important in the calendars of its participants as any other activities.

Moreover, it affords the most exhilarating of all sports or pastimes, as much to the one who rides in pursuit of hounds as to the one who cannot afford to ride and comes out on foot or bicycle (and who may in fact see more of hounds than the rider). Hunting seems to foster a spirit of comradeship and understanding between all people which is very valuable, and it also appears to keep the numbers of foxes in the countryside in check with no more pain and suffering than they would suffer from destruction by alternatives such as trapping, poisoning or gassing.

However, it is no part of our object to descend into abstract discussion of the sport, but rather to consider the part we intend to play in it. There are few hunting countries where a keen beginner is not sure of a warm welcome and, once the first introductions are made, a circle of acquaintance and friendship will soon develop.

But the beginner has certain obligations, as does any member of a hunt. To maintain a hunt establishment costs more and more as the years go by and it is a fact that many hunts would have languished and disappeared in recent years had it not been for substantial contributions in terms of time and effort contributed over and above the basic subscriptions. Accordingly, the first duty of the aspiring fox-hunter is to ensure that the appropriate subscription is paid punctually, and that any help that is required with other fund-raising activities is given.

If you live in the area in which you intend to hunt you probably know it well—though nothing like so well as you will know it in a couple of seasons' time! If you are a newcomer to the country you must somehow make the time to get down and learn a little about it and the people who live in it, and get known yourself. The hunting season proper is from the first of November to about the end of March, depending on the springtime weather, with a couple of months' cub-hunting before and the odd bye-day and point-to-points after.

Do not make the mistake of thinking that the hunt is inactive for the rest of the year for in many ways the summer months are as strenuous for the hunt committee and hunt servants as the months of the hunting season. Apart from considerations of kennel and stable there are the local shows, the Pony Club (and most Pony Club branches are attached to the local hunt) and, above all, the Master's job of 'keeping the country sweet' by constant attentions to social matters, such as the Farmers' Dinner and all the little things which help to keep him in touch with what is going on in the neighbourhood. In these tasks, as with fund raising, anyone who hunts can help and so enhance sport and lighten the work of those who provide it.

Unless you know the individual hounds who compose the pack with which you hunt you are missing a good half of the fun. The foxhound, as well as being a thing of beauty, is a strong and attractive individualist, even though his life is essentially a communal one.

At first glance it seems that it would be impossible ever to tell the thirty-five or forty members of a hunting pack apart. Many who know the best of hunting regard the knowledge of, and interest in, hounds as being infinitely more important than the ability to follow them on

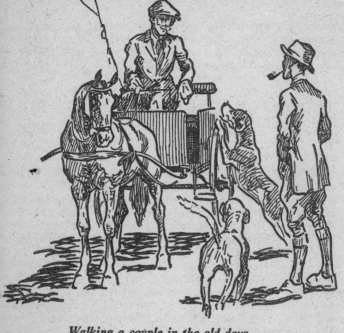

Walking a couple in the old days...

horseback or on foot. And by knowing the hounds you
may often gain the information that gives you a priceless
start in a memorable run. It is regrettably a fact that
many of those who would most indignantly deny any
imputation that they are not real foxhunters are
abysmally ignorant of the hounds on whom they depend
for their sport.

If you live in the country and have the time and place,
it is a duty as well as a great pleasure to 'walk' a puppy,
or even a couple, for the Master. This means that you will
bring up the pup from the time he is weaned from his dam

Don't gallop amongst stock

until he is ready to join the rest of the pack for cub-hunting at the beginning of his first season.

It is an endless source of pleasure, not to say pride, to see your 'own' hound hunting with the rest of the pack when he has reached maturity. There are also the hunt servants, huntsman, kennel-huntsman, whippers-in, grooms and kennelmen, each of whom is a key person in his own sphere. If you wish to enjoy your sport you must get to know all of them and be their friend. It is useful to keep in touch with as many farmers as you can and to get to know their stockmen and labourers too, in fact, every-one who is even remotely concerned with the hunt. Un-obtrusively endeavour to identify yourself with your country and you will be helping its life and its problems and, incidentally, making your own life really worth living.

'Hunting manners'—or etiquette—are simply good man-ners, the basic civility with which all countrymen from the largest landowner to the farmworker are generously endowed. We ride after hounds over other people's land, from which they extract their living, at their implicit invitation, and common sense and decency dictate that they should not be the sufferers thereby. Obviously, then, we must avoid doing anything that will harm the land or the crops and stock that are raised on it.

As to gates, the rule is that the last one through checks that the gate or rails are closed, irrespective of the delay. If gaps are left open, valuable animals may stray and be

Get his quarters into the hedgerow

injured, and why should the farmer pay his men to spend time searching for stock and bringing them home? Never gallop among farm animals, and especially among breeding stock and milking cows. Counsels of perfection demand that you should slow to a walk in a field where stock are turned out, but at least keep away from them and reduce your pace if they are obviously upset.

Avoid damage to fences by unnecessary jumping, for to repair a broken fence costs time and money which will probably have to come from hunt funds. Report any breakages to the hunt secretary and be prepared to pay yourself to have them made good. Never ride over seeds, or indeed any growing crop, but 'ride the headlands' or, if possible, avoid such fields altogether.

Actually, a single horse or, for that matter, a line of them abreast will usually do less harm, except in really wet weather, than the more usual 'line ahead'. And never fail to pass the time of day with the tractor driver, cowman or odd-jobber you pass, nor neglect the common civility of a 'thank you' when someone opens a gate for you, however hard hounds are running. Galloping past pedestrians and covering them with mud is also offensive and does nothing for the reputation of your sport—after all, how would you like it?

At the meet, always greet the Master with an affable 'Good Morning, Master', and either lift your hat or smile, and at the end of the day remember to say 'Good Night' to him. Greet the huntsman by his name—'Mister' if you are a newcomer—and also the whipper-in and any other hunt staff you meet, who will be known by their Christian names. Remember that you are just one member of the field and do not have any prior rights over anyone else, so take your turn at the gates and gaps and take your turn, too, in getting awkward or broken gates open, even if it means dismounting. If somebody else is doing it for you do not rush off and leave them trying to re-mount a wildly prancing horse, but wait until they are safely back in 'the plate'. Keep well away from hounds and refrain from riding on top of the huntsman, 'in his pocket'. He and his hounds must be given plenty of room if they are to hunt their fox successfully.

If you are riding a kicker . . .

If you cannot get right out of their way, always turn your horse's head towards the hounds and get his quarters into the hedgerow: if you don't he may kick or tread on a hound and make you very unpopular. And hang out the thong of your whip, for hounds understand what this means and will give you a wide berth.

The hunting field is not the place to school a young horse, and if you are riding a 'green' one, a novice hunter, keep well out of everyone else's way, even at the expense of your own enjoyment. If you are so unfortunate as to be riding a kicker, decorate his tail with a red ribbon, and keep to the back of the field.

A well-recognised signal that a horse is sensitive about others coming up behind him is to put your hand behind your back—it indicates that a little caution is advisable for those behind you. But, best of all, get rid of such horses, for hunting is essentially a sociable activity and not the place for anti-social equines.

If you intend to joint a hunt, your approach should be through the secretary, preferably with an introduction from someone who is already a member. Subscribers pay an annual subscription and a small sum as 'field money' on the days on which they go out.

Non-subscribers are charged a more substantial 'cap'

Paying Field Money

as a sort of day membership fee, and they are also expected
to pay field money; if you intend to hunt as a non-sub-
scriber you should, of course, ask the secretary's or
Master's permission to do so, and check whether or not
the number of days on which you may hunt on this basis
is limited.

Do not wait for the secretary to come and ask for 'cap'
or 'field money', but seek him out and pay it at once,
introducing yourself if necessary. When Christmas comes
round do not forget that you owe the hunt servants a
Christmas box; make it as generous as possible, and just
slip it in with the Christmas card which you send. If you
find that you cannot manage a respectable tip all round,
send your mite to the secretary 'for the hunt staff' and he
will see that it gets to the right place.

With the Devon and Somerset

Horse and Hound

Different hunting countries demand different qualities of the hunter, as they do of the foxhound. Indeed, the qualities are often rather similar for both.

For instance, the heavy ploughlands of Essex call for considerable strength and stamina from the hound and his speed is of less importance than his 'nose' and persistence in seeking the line, and the hunter will also require strength and cunning if he is to deal with the continually heavy ground and often tricky fences. In the grass countries of the Midlands a lighter hound with greater speed is nearer to the ideal, and in horses quality is essential, nothing but a thoroughbred giving the speed and boldness that is needed if you are to remain on top of the hunt from start to finish in the Shires and the stone-walled country of the Dukeries. In the Fell countries of the North, where followers fare better on foot than on horses, a quite different hound is employed, lighter and less compact in frame, but with enormous scope and endurance and with the 'hare-foot' and well-developed dew claws which will enable him to cover the rocks and screes of the high hills. In the Devon and Somerset country it is different yet again; a strong, short-legged horse, but still with basic quality, will carry you best where a long-legged, keen and excitable thoroughbred would be as likely to let you down as to show you the best of the hunt. And the horse is not the only consideration.

'Know thyself' is the most valuable advice in life. The aim of the aspiring fox-hunter should be to obtain a horse that will suit the rider and in selecting a horse it is most important to keep the rider's abilities and limitations in mind. We ride in order to hunt, to see the sport and to keep with hounds while they are running. Some people, to be sure, hunt to ride and to them the accent is entirely on the riding. Many such would be hard put to it to give a coherent account of a day's sport, although they can most accurately describe every obstacle they jumped over—or through—from start to finish.

If we go hunting to hunt and see hounds at work, we shall miss much of the fun if all our attention has to be devoted to controlling the horses we bestride, to the

Do not be trapped into overhorsing yourself

exclusion of everything else. A careless, excitable, beast with no manners could easily give you so much trouble that you miss all the sport, so do not be trapped into over-horsing yourself or you may well regret it. On the other hand, a hunter must be able to gallop and jump, and be keen to do it, and he must be 'sound' in wind and limb if he is to do his job.

For the beginner who intends to hire a horse, it is well to make the appropriate connections well before the season, or even cub-hunting, begins. In many neighbourhoods will be found establishments who cater for those who cannot keep their own horses. Always go to the best and put your case, without reservations, to the proprietor. It is his business and, in his own interests, he will usually serve you as well as he can.

When it comes to buying a horse, it is as well to have a clear notion of what you really need. You will not get it unless you are prepared to pay a good price but if you keep your ideal animal in mind you stand a fair chance of getting something like it. Certain defects of conforma-tion, manners or performance can be improved by careful handling or overcome by good horsemanship but bad temper and physical unsoundness are to be avoided for in most cases they are too deep-seated to be eradicated.

Caveat Emptor

Do not trust to your own judgement or pretend an ability and experience which you do not possess, but enlist the help of a knowledgeable friend, although it should not be forgotten that few people will admit that they are not knowledgeable when it comes to dealings with horses or cars.

It is always a sensible precaution to get a veterinary surgeon's opinion about a horse before you buy it, for he will be able to tell you about its physical state and give advice as to whether, in his view, it is suitable for the purpose for which you are considering buying it. And don't forget any horse worth his salt will be a good deal more keen and excitable out hunting than he is when you try him in the paddock, and allow for that. A reputable dealer or an honest private seller will not mislead you but he is, after all, selling the animal and the rule *Caveat emptor*, or 'buyer beware', is always applicable, especially as dealing with horses seems to bring out a dishonest streak in the most unexpected people.

Hunters are 'let down' slowly at the end of the season, becoming less and less fit until they are ready to be turned out to grass for the summer. Obviously it takes some time for a horse to return to full fitness after this summer holiday and more horses are ruined by being returned to the rigours of the hunting field before they are fully fit again than by any other cause. Adequate preparation, slowly and steadily, is what is required and it is a sensible rule that this should begin on the first of August with light exercise, plenty of steady walking and never more than an occasional slow trot or canter, which will gradually develop muscle in place of fat and accustom him to the change in regime of work and feed.

As far as feed is concerned, do not be trapped into thinking that large quantities of concentrated food will be required at this early stage, for it is the work that is most important throughout the process of getting the horse, like any athlete, 'hard'. Later you will be able to take your horse cub-hunting, although the Master's permission should always be sought first for this period belongs to him alone and it is during this time that he concentrates on teaching the young hounds their business and on welding the pack into an efficient, keen, entity which will hunt foxes well. A crowd of riders out cub-hunting distracts the attention of the 'young entry' and makes the huntsman's job that much more difficult.

While you are giving your horse plenty of hacking about the countryside you will also have a chance to improve your knowledge of its topography, and to note for future reference possible lines which you might take across it, and also the parts which are obviously impassable. In addition, there is no better time than late summer to stop and pass the time of day with the country people you meet, the casual wayfarer and the farm-worker. Apart from other considerations this helps the spirit of unity and comradeship, and a gossip, besides being interesting in itself, will often furnish you with valuable local information.

It should be the object of any rider to bring in the horse, whether from a hack, a hunt, an endurance ride, a trial or a show, enhanced in value and there are many little lessons that can be learned by horse and rider during the casual hack which will result in greater efficiency all round when they take the field. A little schooling in basic dressage and over smallish, solid, jumps in the paddock will not come amiss but be very careful not to overdo it. Later on during the cub-hunting season, as the ground gets cooler in October and scent improves, and when the young hounds have settled down to their task, there are likely to be some respectable runs which will round off the preparation of you and your horse. But remember that the golden rule is to take a horse home too early rather than too late, for it is when horse and rider are tired that accidents happen and that slight extra strain on a muscle or tendon may be just too much when it is already over-fatigued. There are few things more disheartening than to lame your carefully prepared hunter just before the opening meet.

It is essential to your enjoyment and to that of others that your horse should be completely in control and both willing and able to answer promptly all the aids that you give him. A horse that will not, for example, go about the business of opening and shutting a gate is a nuisance and liable adversely to affect your popularity out hunting. In these simple manœuvres you will find yourself asking for a rein-back, turn on the haunches, centre or forehand. These are all important lessons and your hacks in the country give a good opportunity to perfect them.

A horse that will not stand still to be mounted or at the covert-side is also a pest, but patience and practice will eventually get him to obey. Most horses from a riding school or a hiring establishment are unwilling to leave others and few are keen to turn away from a line of their comrades if you decide to go your own way. But if your mount cannot be made to do these things your sport will certainly suffer, for grand opportunities will certainly be missed. Occasionally, one comes on horses which are reluctant to walk down steep slopes unless they are led, and again plenty of opportunities fo_ practice arise while hacking, and your rides need never be dull. But a horse, like his rider, is liable to boredom and will lose patience and temper if any one training exercise is continued for too long.

When the horse has developed some muscle, and 'hardened' a little as he begins to get fit, an occasional gallop will help him, and you will both enjoy it as well as

Cross his front legs . . .

its doing you good. The daily period of exercise to aim
for is about two hours, although this is not always practicable, and it is a good practice to walk the first half mile
away from the stables and the last mile back to them
again, to ensure that the animal is not brought in sweating
and excited.

Remember, too, that when you rise at the trot your
weight is in the air for one diagonal and in the saddle for
the other, and if you do not use the horse's two diagonals
approximately equally the horse can get very one-sided.
Indeed, many horses have already developed rather one-
sidedly so that they find it very uncomfortable if the rider
sits on the unaccustomed diagonal, and will sometimes
change pace or shy to make it more comfortable. 'Chang-
ing diagonals' is simple enough, by sitting for two strides
instead of one, and though it may feel strange at first you
should be sure to use both diagonals equally.

At canter and gallop a horse may, if he is allowed to
have all his own way, develop a favourite lead so be sure
that you always indicate which one you have chosen, and
insist that he uses it. If you do not you could even suffer

a fall on the flat as the horse, if he is leading with the outside leg as he goes round a bend, can quite easily cross his front legs and fall over them, which is very humiliating.

In this mechanical age too many people are liable to regard a horse as a mere vehicle. Remember that he is a sentient, alert and moderately intelligent creature, and enjoys society just as much as we do. And, although his herd instinct naturally draws him to equine companions, he seems to appreciate human friendship almost as much. So visit him when you can, either in his stable or turned out in the field. He does not understand our complex language but the tone of voice can convey some meaning to him, and talking to your horse will always improve your relationship with him.

'The English Hunting Seat'

Not so long ago, England was largely unenclosed. In Beckford's time, for instance, the Enclosures Act was still far away, but hunting the fox was already a national pursuit, and one which was very necessary since overgrowth of the fox population would have led to serious depredations on both farmers' stock and on the poultry which everyone, from the poorest labourer to the wealthy landowner, kept in the backyard and relied upon for the eggs which in many cases constituted an essential part of the human diet.

The accent on pace and riding after hounds came later when hunting developed into a fashionable sport during the nineteenth century. Before then, hounds drew up to their fox on his drag and having made him get up and away proceeded to hunt him persistently and slowly, if effectually, with their noses and would only occasionally run in view.

With the coming of the enclosures and the increasing wealth of England, and rural England too, the development of the high-class English thoroughbred and the fashion for fast and dangerous field sports, hunting became a specialised undertaking, with the accent on pace and riding, rather than being an entirely rural pastime indulged in by all and sundry. The effect was an increase

The accent on speed developed during the XIX Century

in the science of the chase and in the amount of help that hounds could expect from their huntsman, the improvement of hound and horse as they were bred for quality and speed, and the development of a tradition that the cost of hunting makes it a pastime of the 'aristocracy'. The later plutocracy helped to nurture this idea in their own interests, and the belief persists even now although hunting has, as a result of the enormous cost of keeping a pack of hounds, returned to the simplicity of a better age.

What with the prevalence of wire as a fencing material in modern agriculture, the necessary seclusion of disease-free herds of farm animals, the overgrown state of our woods and coverts and the breaking up of our ancient pastures, there are few countries today where you can ride as hard as you dare in any direction; indeed there are some who would argue, and some of their reasoning is undeniably valid, that modern agriculture has put fox-hunting in the position of an indefensible anachronism. Yet there are as many people hunting today as ever there were, probably more, and most hunt for the love of hunting and not solely for the purpose of riding across country. If the latter is your main wish you will anyway get much pleasure from competitive events, such as hunter trials and combined training events, or from drag-hunting, where the pace is guaranteed to be hot and the fences on the 'line' are sure to be free of wire.

The foregoing may seem a trifle irrelevant, but it does provide the background for the evolution of the traditional English 'hunting seat' and its modern derivatives.

The English 'hunting seat' was, and for many still is, the basis of English horsemanship for generations and has adapted to its purpose well as it developed over the years. It provided a style of riding which virtually any rider, irrespective of age and physical fitness, could adopt on any horse, schooled or not, the slowest most solemn cob or the hot-headed ex-racehorse, and would permit the rider to go over any country, fast or slow, fenced or not. It would also provide that rider with the control and security that is required for hunting. Of course, there were exaggerated variants which we see less and less to-

Once, you could ride in any direction

Exaggerated variants of

the early XX Century

day, but although these were often pictured, most knowledgeable riders took them for what they were.

The English 'hunting seat' owed much of its strength to
the cavalry style of riding which had great influence on
horsemen in Britain during the first half of the twentieth
century, not surprisingly, since a large proportion of the
men who hunted then would have served at one time or
another in an army which still used horses extensively.

Traditional styles for riding across country have been
modified by the increasing accent on competitive riding
and the improvement in quality and training of all the
horses that we ride. Now that the horse is seldom required
simply as a means of transport his intrinsic value has
increased and he is always a possession to be treasured

To keep your position

nowadays, the more so because of the cost of keeping the individual animal. The improvement in veterinary treatment also means that many injuries which would in earlier days have led to chronic lameness, and thus by implication a bullet, can be successfully treated so that there is smaller risk of all that careful training being wasted literally with the slip of a foot. The continental school of equitation introduced a riding style that is based on a theoretically acceptable position and proper balance of the rider on the horse's back, rather than pure tradition. It is now so commonly seen in the show-jumping arena and at combined training events that it seems difficult to imagine that once it was considered *very* innovative, something that could never edge its way into the hunting field. But it has, to the benefit of both horses and riders.

Naturally, in the hunting field you will be faced with more 'emergencies' in the course of a day than will occur during a week of hacking. Also, you hope, you will be riding across country at a reasonably rapid pace, a brisk canter or gallop, and leaping the natural obstacles that come in your path. You will probably find it advisable to shorten your stirrup leathers a hole or two from the length which is comfortable for hacking. This must not result in the rider being less 'into' the saddle than before, but it should give a little extra grip when it comes to jumping.

It is worth remembering when you are jumping in the hunting field that although the fences may not be as large and terrifying in appearance as those met in competitive cross-country riding, no-one has been round and removed the old tree stumps and broken gates from the other side. Nor can you be sure that the ground is smooth. There may well be holes and ruts on the other side, so that there is a tendency to go 'with' the horse and adopt a 'forward' position a little less, so that if he does slip or stumble on landing, or indeed as he gallops, you will be able to keep your position.

The ideal is to be able to keep your attention on what hounds are doing when they are in sight and to note the various signs which indicate the line of country you are most likely to have to ride over. You will also need to keep your eyes on the route a field or two ahead of

Out of your way, wet and cold

where you are, in order to keep and find your direction. Thus very much must be left to the horse, though you must be ready to help him when he needs it, to steady him and make him time his leaps properly and to save him from taking too much out of himself. To do this your position in the saddle must be firm but readily adaptable, and of course the saddle itself should be of the 'general purpose' type which will not fix you in any set style as, for example, a show jumping saddle—which has a higher pommel and candle—would do.

There are very few countries now where one can follow one's own line, and we are told that anyway there were always a good fifty riders in any field to every one who did so. And unless you are very careful, and really know the people over whose land you are riding, the Master and secretary will not thank you for breaking away from the rest of the field and possibly breaking agreements which they have made with landowners. None the less, when you rise to that level of competence there is no denying that it is much more satisfying to ride one's own line after hounds, rather than joining in the game of 'follow-my-leader' with the rest of the field after the field-master. But your first few times out it is a good idea to select a pilot, someone who has many years' of experience in the hunting field behind him, although he may be inconspicuous in general turnout and mounted on a horse whose reputation depends more on his brains than his looks.

If you follow your pilot from a respectful distance, and ensure that it is not obvious that you are using him as such, you may well find that the line he chooses, though less exciting and perhaps including a considerable amount of road-riding, may bring you closer to hounds for more of the time than your own unaided efforts and knowledge of the country could ever have done.

While considering knowledge of the country, it is a good idea to carry with you, during your hacks about the countryside and also when you take the field, a fairly large scale Ordnance Survey map. This will allow you to check your position frequently when out for a ride, and should help you to avoid getting lost while out hunting as you may well do, especially at the end of a run. Local information is often unreliable particularly as it is often hardest to get the route from someone who really knows it well. You may well find yourself miles out of your way, wet and cold, with a tired horse and no idea where you are. The end of Mr. Jorrocks's bye-day with Charley Stobbs is an awful warning, and who of us has not experienced the same? An extra advantage that you will enjoy if you use a large scale map—and it needs to be large enough to show the individual fields—is that you can go over the day's sport again at your leisure and, one hopes, re-live all its pleasures if not its pains.

The Opening Day
However, here you are at the opening meet on the first Saturday of November, all eager for the fray though un-

doubtedly a shade nervous as to how you will acquit yourself. One comfort is that there are bound to be several other riders out who are equally inexperienced in the field. This is a great moment:

'. . . Delightful scene!
When all around is gay, men, horses, dogs;
And in each smiling countenance appears
Fresh blooming health, and universal joy.'

Give yourself plenty of time to get there, whether you hack on to the meet or go by horsebox. If you box, park at least half a mile away from the place where the meet is to be held and hack on; this will settle your horse and warm him up, and avoid your vehicle getting in everybody's way. But whenever the meet is within reasonable reach, hack out. Hack steadily on the road, and do not hurry. Hunt horses are seldom sick or sorry and think of the enormous distances they cover in the course of a day's hunting. One reason for this is that they are not overfed, and are well exercised at a steady pace, for though it is the 'hammer, hammer, hammer on the hard, high road' that knocks a horse up, the hound-jog or walk will never hurt him. Don't take your horse too near the hounds or you may start your day wrong by treading on one, but manage to get a good look at them and try to identify those you know.

Soon the Master will give the word to move off. There is no hurry, for he will give his field plenty of time, so do not press on the hounds' sterns, but take your place among the rest of the field, keeping your pilot well in sight. Stay with the crowd, as directed by the field-master, if there is one, close by the covert-side and keep still and silent from the moment the hounds enter to covert to draw for their fox. If you see a member of the field going off on his own, do not follow him, for, in all probability he has gone on some errand for the Master. Avoid 'coffee-housing', for chatter and restive horses will distract hounds quicker than anything.

If your horse begins to play up, take him away until you can quieten him. Listen for the first whimper from a hound: later you may be able to distinguish the voice of each hound and form your own conclusions, but that time is not yet. There they go at last, a full-throated chorus, but wait still, for they may hunt him in covert for half an hour yet before they put him away and if you dash off wildly you may head the fox back into covert. A shrill screech from a whipper-in posted on the far side of the covert tells you that the fox has 'gone away'. Keep your head and your horse in hand, for hounds must be given room to settle to their line before you go after them.

For the first few minutes most of your efforts will be expended in keeping your horse in control and steadying him, for the greatest slug that ever was foaled will show signs of excitement when hounds begin to run and other horses are galloping. And here, keep cool, and steady him by a light give-and-take of your hands and by speaking to him quietly. Don't shout at him or haul at his mouth, for this will make him worse than ever and he may never settle down at all. Remember that from now on you will have to look after yourself and keep your eyes open for loose wire, rabbit holes and other *imponderabilia*, as well as refraining from getting in the way of other riders and foot followers.

Jumping, you will soon find, is a different business from jumping in the school or paddock, where the obstacles are bound to be straightforward and on the level. Such jumps out hunting are the exception rather than the rule. Here comes the first one, a low stake and bind: sit down, grip tight, steady your horse to a canter, even a trot, and then drive him to it with pressure from seat-bones to heel. Give him his head as he comes into it and over you go, resuming your normal position as he lands. Don't get 'left behind', for a jab in the mouth as he takes off is the surest way to upset a horse's balance (to say nothing of your own) and it may throw him down. Most experienced hunters are pretty capable of taking care of themselves and of you, and will correct a faulty approach or a mistake on your part by 'putting in a short one' or a scramble. Be ready for it.

The hardest thing of all is to refrain from trying to remedy a peck on landing by a pull on the reins. Left

The greatest slug ever foaled will show signs of excitement

alone a horse will nearly always save himself, probably
by the use of his nose and neck as his 'fifth leg', but he
cannot do so if you haul his head up just when he needs
to get it down. Only experience and the confidence given
by an unshakable seat will enable you to do this automatically.

Here comes the next one, a thorn hedge, but the man
in front has disappeared and it didn't look like a fall:
no it wasn't, there he goes, it's a drop. Steady your horse
again and be ready for what is coming. As he rises recover
your upright position, letting your reins slip and as he
comes down lean back without shifting your legs, and
there you are on the right side again.

What's that? They seem to have stopped in front; it is
a check in the next field.

Without waiting for a 'hold-hard' from anyone, stop at
once and keep still and silent, while hounds feather and
try to find the line again. The chances are that the fox has
turned sharp along the hedgerow. One hound speaks, the
others join him and confirm his news. Off they go again,
but wait for them, for the quarry may have turned back
again and by riding parallel with the hounds you may
cross and foil his line. No; there they go. Is his point that
covert on the hillside a mile or so away? Yes; see those
bullocks in the field bunching together, heads all pointing
in the same direction.

C

The riders in front have pulled sharp aside from the next fence. It must be wire and they are making for the gateway by those tree trunks and the sooner you are after them the better. Here we are on a road, but there is a grass verge so get on to it and you can gallop after them. Presently a few turn off up a lane, but your unconscious pilot continues along the road. The chances are he knows the best way; perhaps all the fields are wired just here.

Yes, he knew; there he goes now through a gate into that next field. He turns to see if any follow, lift your whip to show that you are coming too and as you come to the open gate look round in your turn. No one is coming; you must shut the gate. Here are seeds so you must ride round the field as your pilot is doing. Here is a gap and you avoid it, so as not to increase it, and jump at a more solid spot; hounds are still running hard two fields ahead, but there is nobody with them. Another small jump, but with a ditch beyond and your horse, not having been pressed at it, drops his hind legs into it and you are on his neck.

A gate, a scramble over a bank and you are just in time to see the tail hounds crash into the covert.

Your companion calls to you to look after the left side of the covert and goes in after the pack. The hounds' cry dies down to a mere whimper and you halt level with them to await events. Soon there is silence. Still you wait, keeping close to the covertside and looking behind you as well as in front.

Suddenly a screech from a jay in front; what is that small brownish object a hundred yards on? Yes, it is the fox: he pauses to look round and you keep deathly still.

Finally he makes off at an easy lope, clearly not distressed, but he looks a shade bedraggled and it must be the hunted fox. What to do now? Common sense supplies the answer and off you go to the point where he came out of the covert and then essay your first holloah—in what you hope (erroneously) is a fair imitation of Tom's rendering when he went away turning your horse in the direction the fox went and lifting your hat. Nothing happens for minutes until a hound appears nose down

.. and you're on his neck

and stern up just inside the wood. Leave him alone, for
he is doing his job and needs all his faculties, and you
recognise him as old Challenger, one of the few you know
and a notable hunter.

Just as you wonder what on earth to do next up comes
the huntsman in a lather. Don't enter into a lengthy dis-
course on viewing your first fox, but simply say, 'he went
down that hedgerow as far as I could see him and he
left five minutes ago'. Don't add the usual fallacious, but
almost invariable 'information' that he is 'dead-beat', because he obviously wasn't and in any case you wouldn't
know.

A note on the horn, a cheer, and here come the pack,
converging from all points of the compass to its summons.
Challenger is leading down the hedgerow, with a deep
'ough, ough', and soon the pack score to his cry. By
this time the field, having been held up by wire, are
coming up and your brief moment of glory is over.

Off they go again, sinking into the vale below. No
longer can you see your pilot: now it's up to you. A few
in front press on, and the rest turn sharp left down an
overgrown track, but you decide to hold on. Soon a line
of rails confronts you, a solemn moment, for they are
high and look solid. One of the men in front is down,

breaking a top rail in the process; another refuses, but
the fallen warrior is up again and, taking advantage of
his misfortune and steadying to a trot, you put your horse
to it and, with a firm urge, over you go. Thank goodness
for that broken panel!

Next, in a line of wire, comes an uncompromising gate
a full five feet high. The girl in front, obviously an expert,
makes a perfect leap, but you share neither her skill nor
her mount, and discretion is obviously the better part.
Having learned his lesson, your horse obeys your commands and somehow you get it open. Anybody coming:
yes, so on again, but now there is no one in sight to
follow, nor any vestige of hounds or field. You neither
know the country nor the point for which the fox is
making, but there is another road running roughly in the
direction you think is the line. You listen and look, but
no sign of anything, so let's get on, in the hope of finding
hounds. Half an hour's solitary trot and a car follower
tells you which way they have gone and, if you are lucky,
the best way to get to them. Soon you see a few more
foot followers and a car or two drawn up beside that big
wood and presently signs of the hunt. You have been
lucky to get up to them, for they have just lost their fox
in this big stronghold and presently they have to give up.
The next move is still farther away from your base and a
long draw proves blank.

After some debate the Master decides to move on, a
move which would take you still farther from home and
rest, the sun is getting low and your horse is showing
signs of having had enough—after all it is the first day
of the season—so, sadly but wisely, you decide to call it
a day and set off on your homeward way having bid the
Master and your companions 'goodnight'. You have but
the vaguest idea where you are, but take the road that
seems best for you and after an hour's walking and slow
trotting you begin to see landmarks you feel that you
recognise, and a sign confirms that you are on the right
road. Keep at a steady walk or jog with an occasional
trot to prevent the horse from getting cold and stiff, and
you will find that if you walk or jog beside him he will
appreciate the rest, and it will keep you—especially your

At an easy lope

Thank goodness for that broken panel

feet—warm, too. A drink will do him no harm now that he has cooled off, and he will be grateful for it.

Another hour and you are back at the horsebox, and you are glad that you took the time and trouble this morning to park in a lay-by where you could re-load out of the way of motor traffic, for it is getting dark now and you and your muddy horse do not show up well. The horse seems almost to recognise the vehicle, for he pricks up his ears and quickens his pace as it comes in view. You have no-one there to help you but the animal seems only too willing to co-operate by standing still while you slacken the girths and shift the saddle on his back before his blanket and rug are thrown over him. It is not a very long drive home, and there is plenty of bedding in the box, so you do not bother with leg bandages, although it is wise to put a bandage round his tail in case he rubs it, and you are glad that you remembered to bring a spare one, ready rolled up, this morning. Last of all, the bridle is replaced with a headcollar, and you gratefully load yourselves up for the journey home.

On arriving home the first job is to settle the horse in

Bidding your companions goodnight

his stable. Check that he is warm by feeling his ears—
they should be warm right to their tips—and that he is
dry, and rub with clean straw any patches which are damp
with mud or sweat. It is also important to make sure
that circulation has been fully restored to areas where
harness has exerted pressure, especially under the saddle,
so give these a good brushing and try to get the worst off
the rest of him quickly.

There is little point, however, in spending a long time
grooming him at this stage, for it will only tire both of
you more and the dirt will come off much more easily in
the morning. Like you, your horse is tired and hungry,
and wants a good meal and then a chance to lie down
and rest on a deep bed. He also needs warm, dry, clothing,
so do not put the sweaty, damp, rug and blanket that you
used earlier back on him, but find him dry ones, and you
might add some loose stable bandages too if the weather
is cold. You will have to use your common sense about
how much clothing you put on him, for there is no need
to cook him, but he does need to be warm and comfortable. He will feel the cold a little more when he is tired
that he would normally do. While this is going on the
horse can have some hay to pick at and when you have
finished your chores, which should include going over
him for small injuries and checking that his feet are clean,
he will probably appreciate a drink of warm gruel, made
by pouring hot water onto oatmeal.

Alternatively, you could give him some warm water
(for some strange reason known in equestrian tradition
as 'chilled' water), but make sure that he has satisfied his
thirst before he is given his main feed. Then he can be
left while you go in for that delicious hot bath and meal.
But do not forget the horse, for he will need a couple of
visits later in the evening to check that he is well and
comfortable before you say 'goodnight' to him too.

It wasn't so very terrible after all, was it? You have
had a good hunt, seen the quarry, and done your part as
a fox-hunter and you should be eager for the next day's
sport. Your horse has carried you well and seems to have
suffered no harm from the physical exertion, although—
like you—he was a trifle stiff the next day, and you feel

Grooves his legs for injuries

that your decision to buy him has been well vindicated.
You seem to be making satisfactory progress towards
your firm aim, which is to become independent of guides
and advice, knowledgeable of the country, and always
ready to help those in need of it.

Falls
'A fall's a h'awful thing', said John Jorrocks at one of
his 'Sportin' lectors', and so it is, but seldom so awful as
one imagines it to be, when once one has learned how
to do it.

There used to be a saying to the effect that nobody
would ever learn to ride without taking some falls in the
process, and there is some truth in this for there are few
beginners who have got through their early teaching without parting company with the horse once or twice, and

The hat that falls off in a fall

even the finest horseman rider in the world may hit the
ground if a horse is brought down. But any competent
instructor will do all possible to prevent the pupil from
sustaining a fall for it may shake the nerve of a beginner
and put back progress considerably, and confidence is
everything to one who is learning. Once you have had
one or two falls you will discover that, apart from the
initial moment of alarm and general discomfort, the
chances that you will sustain serious damage are in fact
very slim indeed.

'Throw your heart over and follow it as soon as you
can' is another traditional saying that merely implies that
if you really want to get over a fence then you will. 'Look

The best may be brought down

before you leap, but if you intend leaping then don't
look for too long', is another in the same vein, and equally
valuable. If you are not quite determined to go over,
your horse will know it before you do and may hesitate
and either stop or make a mess of the jump. The fool-
hardy rider, to be sure, will take many falls and deserves
them because there is all the world between bravery and
idiotic rashness.

Some people seem almost to enjoy sharp contact with
the ground, but you will find that the bold and experienced rider will have very few falls, if any, during a
season's hunting, irrespective of whether the horse is a
good one or a bad one, because determination to jump
and the ability to give the horse the best possible chance
of getting over make a great difference. Many falls need
not happen. To be sure there are the unavoidable ones,
such as a slip-up on tarmac or through a horse's putting
his foot in a hole or a blind ditch, and these are apt to be
the nastiest, too.

The art of falling is to relax every muscle the moment
you feel you are bound to go. This takes courage, but the
human frame is reasonably pliable when it is not tensed

up and can withstand considerable shock and strain so
that there is a good chance that, apart from a violent
bump as you come to earth, no serious damage will be
sustained. But if you try to save yourself you may put just
that extra bit of strain in the wrong direction that will do
more serious damage. When you feel that you are going,
duck your head and try to time your descent so that you
will fall on a pad of muscle, for example on the back of
your shoulder or your bottom, and most probably you will
come up as good as new.

Never try to break a fall with your arm, a natural
defence, but dangerous. And, of course, whenever you are
riding a horse your head must always be protected with
an approved style of riding hat for—as some of us know
to our cost—severe concussion, especially if sustained
when you are young, can have serious effects many years
later. It is a reflection of the speed at which knowledge, in
general and in the very traditionally minded field of
equitation, is developing, that for the first sixty years of
the twentieth century as the pictures in this book show, it
was *very* uncommon to see riders wearing really effectively reinforced, rather than just 'hard' hats secured with
chin straps which would keep them on in case of a fall
(rather than just to avoid the hats being brushed off by a
branch). Now it is by no means exceptional in Europe,
and those with an iota of sense will realise that is rather
silly to ride without such when it is available. Because
risking brain damage when riding may be traditional,
this does not make it acceptable.

A reliable way of breaking your neck is to land chin
first, and as a basic guide the 'foetal' position is the one
in which you are likely to sustain least harm from a fall.
It is at the small, insignificant places that the worst of
falls happen, but despite this a fall is not a thing to be
feared, though it is best avoided. Many falls are not really
'falls' except in the sense that the victim has quit the
saddle. A horse hates falling and most hunters become
very expert at avoiding it. Here again a strong, independent, seat will enable you to remain in position as
your horse's nose or knees hit the ground, and allow you
to 'slip' the reins and so give him the freedom of his neck,

Land on a pad of muscle

his fifth leg, and you can also help him recover with strong pressure from your legs. Nearly all riding is 'legs, legs, legs,' and again 'legs'. Give your horse his chance and more often than not you will be up and away again in no time.

It would be idiotic to pretend that there is no danger in falling. Of course there is, as there is in all sports. One of the worst of the lot is to be dragged with one foot wedged in a stirrup, having relinquished the reins. So see that your stirrup irons give plenty of freedom to your foot, and avoid having either rubber or projections on the soles of your boots. For this reason leather riding boots are preferable to rubber ones, despite their greater cost, and it is noticeable how much warmer leather boots are, too. It is also possible to buy rubber wedges which will fit over the bar of the stirrup iron; to a good rider these are quite unnecessary, since a steady pressure is maintained on the stirrup all the time and it cannot slip off the rider's foot.

Another prolific source of serious damage is retaining a hold on the reins as the fall develops and thus pulling the horse over onto yourself for, whatever else he may do, any horse will struggle violently to regain his feet as quickly as possible. Many will tell you to hang onto the

—and help him to recover

reins whatever happens but you may find yourself wishing that you hadn't. If it's going to be a proper fall—and that is your only excuse for quitting the saddle—let it all go, and yourself, too. It is loathsome to have to trudge and shamble across heavy plough or wet pasture, in breeches and boots that were designed for riding and not walking, and it is undignified as well, but it is no doubt preferable to 'having 'a great sixteen 'and 'oss lyin' on one like a blanket, or sittin' with his monstrous hemispheres on one's chest, sendin' one's werry soul out of one's nostrils!' Dreadful thought! Usually, some kind person will catch your horse for you anyway, if only as an insurance for an imponderable future, just as you will do the same for any other unfortunate fellow rider.

Finally, let us consider yet another ineffable truth put into the mouth of the immortal Jorrocks by Robert Smith Surtees:

'And here let me observe that, to 'unt pleasantly, two things are necessary—to know your 'oss and to know your own mind.'

And undignified as well

This knowledge will save you grief and sorrow and enhance both your sport and your reputation.

Hunting Manners
Civility and consideration for others are the basis of all good manners, and this applies in the hunting field as much as anywhere else. And because you are riding a horse fast and furious over other people's land, and participating in a traditional English sport, you certainly do not have the right to be offensive or offhand to *anyone* else. Indeed, to be allowed to fox-hunt is a great privilege, and it is a mark of the thinking and knowledgeable rider that he or she is *never* rude or ill-mannered to any other person, whatever the circumstances.

Admittedly, such civility demands a degree of control over your horse and a level of education which many newcomers will not have achieved, and of course a proportion of them never will, for they cannot distinguish between the good manners which will enhance life for all—not only those following hounds—and will improve the hunt's reputation, and the boorish behaviour which is unpleasant to encounter and does immeasurable damage to hunting.

Among fellow riders, remember that hounds, or one hound for that matter, always come first, and it is often helpful to indicate their presence with a call of 'Hounds, please'. The hunt servants and the Master also have right of way, for they have a job to do, and their path should also be cleared with calls of 'Huntsman, please', or 'Whip, please', or 'Master, please', as appropriate. And make sure that you are well out of their way, with your horse's head turned towards them.

Cutting in on other riders and letting gates slam in their faces will obviously make you most unpopular, and it is a matter of common decency to pass on warnings of dangers to others with the calls such as ' 'Ware hole', or ' 'Ware wire', pointing if necessary with your whip. Where you have to take your turn at a place, give the rider in front plenty of room, for nothing upsets a horse more than to have another animal treading on his heels; it will make him nervous and inclined to pull, and rush the one in front of him, and so on right up the line. If your horse refuses, then pull him out and take your place at the end of the queue. Never jump, or 'skylark', unless it is un-avoidable, because you could thus wantonly damage a fence.

A horse that is likely to swerve (and he should not be out hunting until he has been broken of the habit) must be kept wide of the field so as not to interfere with them, for he could be the cause of a bad accident and at best may make other horses refuse. Try also to avoid gallop-ing close past another rider who is having trouble with a horse because it will further excite the intractable quad-ruped, but if you are going to pass from behind give some warning, for example by calling out 'May I come past you?' The other rider can scarcely say 'No', and will at least know that you are coming.

Always catch a loose horse and return it—you never know when you may need the compliment returned—though it is a hard thing to do when hounds are running on a screaming scent. 'Do as you would be done by', is indeed a rule that cannot be bettered in the hunting field, as in life.

As a counsel of perfection you should not hesitate to offer your horse to a hunt servant whose own has gone lame, or is even dead beat. Naturally, you are always ready to dismount to open a gate for hunt staff, or to hold

Riding on another's heel was always unpopular

horses when huntsman and whips have had to enter a
covert on foot to help hounds. And try to remain in the
same place unless you are asked to move away—it can
be disconcerting to come back for one's horse and find it
and the person holding it gone.

It is best not to address huntsman or whip unless he
needs information, in which case he will ask for it, and
never offer advice, or you could be surprised by an unpleasant, even humiliating, reply, well deserved. When
you go home, even if it is early in the day and still broad
daylight, it is customary to say 'Goodnight', and of course
you will make a point of saying this to the Master and
hunt staff if you see them. You should also bid 'Goodnight' to other followers, which include both riders and
foot-followers, and it is a pleasant tradition to make your
farewell to others you meet on the road in the same way.
Concerning the Master, remember that he or she and the
hunt servants all work very hard for your sport, so never
lose a chance to admire an outstanding hound or the
good work of the pack. We all like to receive praise where
it is due.

There are many children hunting now, and although they can be a nuisance at times remember that you were a child yourself once, so be patient with them and, instead of shouting at them or cursing under your breath, take a later opportunity to speak quietly and kindly to the offender. The chances are that the offence will not be repeated and, after all, every novitiate makes mistakes at some time. It is helpful if you know exactly what the calls on the horn and terms used in hunting mean, and a list of them is given below: —

Drawing Covert	————
Fox on Foot	u u u u u u u
Gone Away } Kill and Worry }	u u u / u u u / u u u
To Ground	- - - / - - - / - - -
Blowing out of Covert	————————
All hounds on	———— u
'Ware heel or riot	u ————
Home	∿∿∿ / ∿∿∿

The Fox

Dog fox	= male.
Vixen	= female.
A brace of foxes	= two foxes.
A leash of foxes	= three foxes.
Mask	= head.
Pad	= foot.
Brush	= tail.
Cubs	= young foxes.
An earth	= a hole in which the fox lives.

The Hound

A couple	= two

A matter of common civility

The Hound (cont)

A couple and a half (never 'three')	= three
Dog pack.	
Bitch pack.	
Mixed pack	= dogs and bitches running together.
Running heel	= running back on the line.
Running mute	= running without cry.
Riot	= hunting rabbit, hare or deer.
Feathering	= pack spreading out to recover the scent.
Carrying a good head	= pack running in a compact body.
Young entry	= first season young hounds.

The Huntsman

Loo in.

The Huntsman (cont)

    Hoick.

    Wind him.

    Tally ho!

    Tally ho back!
      (pronounced BIKE).

    Gone away.

    View holloa ('holler')   = a shrill scream.

    Hark to.

    Yoi over.

    'Ware riot.

    Hark forward.

    Owning a scent.

The Hunt

    The draw.

    The find.

    Breast-high scent.

    To blow out of covert.

    Check.

    Casting   = Huntsman directs hounds in hope of recovering scent.

    Lifting hounds   = Huntsman collects hounds for a cast.

    To throw up   = hounds deprived of scent throw up their heads.

    Run to ground   = fox has taken refuge in an earth.

    To change (foxes)

    A sinking fox   = tired fox.

    The kill, or death.

    To chop a fox   = to kill a fox before he has a chance to escape.

The Country

A bullfinch	= thick, high hedge, usually of thorn.
Stake and bind	= hedge, levelled with long branches laid horizontally and supported on stakes.
An oxer or double oxer	= hedge with post and rail on one side or on both.
Post and rails.	
A double, in and out	= two obstacles close to each other but with room for a stride or two in between.
A drop fence	= field on landing side lower than on take-off side.
A ditch to, or from, you	= on the take-off or landing side.
A ride	= cleared strip through woodland.
A headland	= uncultivated strip beside hedgerows.
Ridge and furrow.	
'Ware seeds, roots, wire	= 'avoid' seeds, etc.
A wattle	= a hurdle.
A bottom, a ghyll	= small narrow valley.
A hanger	= small wood growing on a steep slope.

Miscellaneous

Capping	= subscription taken up from non-members.
Field Master	= in charge of the field.
Huntsman	= he is sometimes the Master himself, usually professional.

Miscellaneous (cont)

Kennel-huntsman = in charge of the hounds in kennels, feeding, etc.

1st and 2nd Whipper-in.
A runner.
Terrier-man.

To walk a puppy = to take charge in your own home of a puppy before he is old enough to join the pack.

Hunting Dress

Apart from the periodical small vagaries of fashion, hunting dress has been devised as the result of centuries of practical experience. The traditional pattern is the most comfortable and hard wearing under the exacting and often wet and dirty conditions of the chase. Quality in clothing, as in saddlery, may be a more costly outlay but in the long run it is usually cheaper for the clothes will last longer, and they will also look smart however much hard wear they have seen. And Shakespeare's advice, 'Costly thy habit as thy purse can buy, but not expressed in fancy; rich not gaudy', applies most appositely to apparel in the hunting field.

If he can afford a subscription that warrants it and if he intends to ride *to* hounds, it is most pleasant for a man to come out in what John Jorrocks described as 'the old red rag'. After all, it is the correct dress for the fox-hunting man, although it is not yet acceptable for women unless they are Masters or amateur huntsmen or whips. For the person who intends to hunt in 'pink', breeches should be white, with white strappings.

Black boots with tops whose colour may vary with personal preference from brown to light, pinkish-yellow are correct, and they should have white garter straps. Whatever their colour, all boots should be on the large side, a full size larger than ordinary shoes, with the soles not too thick and, for your own sake, not too tight over the calf or you will suffer agonies. Spur straps should match the boots, black with top boots, and—like the boots

—should be really well polished. Polishing will extend boots' life and make them waterproof (you may also like to put some ski boot wax round the welts to ensure there is no leakage) if they are leather, and rubber riding boots also benefit from a brush up.

It is correct to wear spurs, even if they are only 'dummies' in the sense that they are very short necked and have no rowels, and in any case for a pursuit as active as hunting should always be filed down so that they are blunt and short. And it should always be borne in mind that spurs are not for holding on by!

The red coat is single-breasted, cut high in the collar and traditionally with four buttons. The 'hunt button', which bears the initials of the hunt's name or its special insignia, should not be worn until you have been invited to do so by the Master. Beneath the coat, which is made of a stout 'melton' cloth which is surprisingly tough and nearly waterproof, you may find that a waistcoat is necessary, and here a little fancy is allowed, the permitted colours ranging from plain canary yellow to buff or a plain red or black check, with brass buttons.

The shirt is not visible but an old fashioned cotton or flannel is usually more comfortable than nylon and other synthetic fabrics since the natural ones do not develop that unpleasant damp feeling.

Your 'hunting tie'—often, and wrongly, described as a stock since stocks are always coloured or patterned—will be of white piqué in most cases, and must be properly tied (something you should practise before the opening day) and secured with an unobtrusive pin. Tradition has it that atop of all comes the hunting topper, properly blocked and able to withstand hard treatment. Its brim is flat and narrow and the crown a shade lower than that of the 'London' topper.

A black coat is correct for either men or women (and it cannot be denied that it is also more becoming for women) and for men it is permissible to wear white breeches, with which top-boots are of course obligatory, as are the rest of the trappings described above. The black coat which a man would wear is cut very much as the red one is, with the same high collar which can be turned up to keep the weather out. Most people who hunt in black prefer, however, to wear the 'butcher' or plain black boots which are customary for most other sorts of riding and with these fawn, buff or even an almost creamy colour of breeches is correct and also much more practical.

Although a man who chooses to wear a black coat, top-boots and white breeches should wear a top-hat to be correct, with a black coat and butcher boots a bowler is the correct headwear. In days which are fortunately past it would have been considered incorrect not to say downright rude for anyone other than Master and hunt servants, and perhaps children, to wear a velvet cap although with the arrival of properly re-inforced and chin strapped caps they are also coming to be accepted in others who ride to hounds.

These notes are written for the edification of the tyro who is more likely to come out in 'ratcatcher', which is not nearly so disreputable as it sounds though it allows for a little more latitude than more formal hunting dress. Breeches can vary from yellowish to fawn and polished butcher boots with black garters and spur straps are perhaps more acceptable than brown boots and straps, though these will do at a pinch. The jacket may be a quiet tweed or check, or of melton cloth in a subtle shade, such as brown, lovatt or grey, with a suitable waistcoat and either a neatly tied buff or cream stock or a tidy shirt with collar and tie. Again, a black bowler—a riding one and not a city bowler—is traditional but a properly strapped hard cap is probably acceptable in most instances. 'Ratcatcher' is also correct and comfortable for hacking, although many people prefer not to bother with spurs, and in summer you may find that jodhpurs and jodhpur boots are more comfortable.

Out hunting you will certainly need gloves, and it looks untidy to ride without them. Leather ones allow a more sensitive feel of the reins, although if it starts to rain you will find that they tend to slip. Under these conditions string ones are more comfortable and it is always a good idea to carry a spare pair of string gloves beneath the saddle flap, held in place by the girth straps. Whatever the fabric of the gloves, they should be amply large enough to allow you to move your fingers freely and to ensure that they do not impede circulation to your fingers, which would make them even colder than they would have been anyway.

If it is raining, mackintoshes may help to keep out the worst of the wet, although some people claim that they are no help in this respect and merely get in the way. This is certainly true, in part at any rate, and a good quality coat will keep you dry anyway, and will not suffer from being soaked, so that you may find it most comfortable to wear your jacket and a mackintosh apron to keep your legs dry; there are few things more depressing in the pouring rain than the feeling that water is trickling down inside of your boots.

For anyone who hunts, but not of course for hacking, it is correct to carry a hunting whip. It is never called a crop—which is something that grows in a farmer's field— and must always be equipped with a thong and lash, for without these it looks ridiculous and it cannot be used for its special purpose, which is to direct hounds, usually away from your horse's heels. This is done by swinging the thong gently to remind hounds that your horse is not familiar with them, but the whip is never to be used for hitting them, or for cracking. Like many things in hunting, the carrying of a whip is largely a matter of tradition, but a pleasant one for all that.

3

POINT-TO-POINT RACING

Steeplechasing originated in the hunting field. The chances are that the first 'chase' of all occurred after a blank day when some young bloods, disappointed with their day's sport, decided to have a 'lark' on the way home. 'Race you to Harewood steeple' might well have been the challenge. The first formal steeplechase is reputed to have been the result of a post-prandial argument as to the respective merits of the horses who had carried their riders with marked success in the hunting field, and the subsequent wager was inevitable in those Corinthian days. The challenge issued and the bet registered, minds were turned to considering the best way to delimit the contest. Obviously it had to be across country from one point to another, so that supporters of the contestants could witness the fun. The most obvious 'points' in a country landscape then would have been the steeples of the village churches, more easily defined and recognised than individual trees, woods or hills since each has its own, indisputable, name. And so was born the steeplechase.

Today's elaborately designed National Hunt Steeplechase and its carefully barbered course is a far cry from the casually arranged contest, and the amount of money bet on modern racing is many, many, times more than any of the single bets of those early times. But those contests soon developed into formal race meetings which are now a sport quite separate from hunting, although traditional terms, such as 'hunter chaser' still crop up in Northern Hunt racing. It is, nonetheless, unrelated to point-to-pointing, most of the National Hunt jockeys being professionals and the horses being trained professionally

Held over a natural country

too. And, of course, the prize money offered is very considerable compared with that collected by even the most successful point-to-pointer.

The first 'point-to-point' races were, like the steeplechases, held over natural country, with the line roughly defined by the nomination of certain obvious landmarks and, for example, a truss of hay placed in the fork of a tree, to be kept on their right or left by the field, as ordered. And although drag-hunting is not intended to be a race, it frequently approaches an early style point-to-point more closely than it does fox-hunting, with a marked line over rideable country and a field composed of riders who wish to ride rather than watch hounds at work.

As the country became more enclosed in earlier times, and the economics of agriculture made the use of more and more wire inevitable, the point-to-point courses were more clearly marked and the fences prepared to an even consistency, with the course clearly indicated with flags. The numbers of spectators increased and it became necessary to provide courses which were visible for their whole length. It was not long before the courses were all grass with made-up fences very similar to those seen in National Hunt racing and nothing like the obstacles encountered in the hunting field. Now we ride in sweaters in racing colours, too, and on racing saddles rather than with the 'hunting dress and hunting saddlery' of those early days. Indeed, a modern point-to-point meeting, or 'Hunt Races',

All the riders are amateurs

is very similar to a steeplechase meeting in most respects, including the size of the crowd which it draws. And this is very important for the money raised by the annual point-to-point is now vital to the solvency of virtually every hunt.

The point-to-point still differs from National Hunt racing in a few respects. All the riders are amateurs, and horses are not professionally trained, although nowadays most are thoroughbreds, bred for the job. All the runners must also have put in a certain, minimum, number of days' hunting in the season, and must be certified by the Master as having done so, although it has to be admitted that some of these days are short and the horses may have seen very little hounds. The course itself remains 'natural' in the sense that it is over enclosed fields and ordinary terrain, rather than being almost completely level, and will not boast rails, only posts and ropes, to keep spectators out of the way. The fences can be taken at speed, for they will contain no hidden traps and are of equal consistency all over, but the pace does not match up to that of the professionals. Nonetheless, the local races provide excellent sport and the annual point-to-point is a

Dwelling at his fences

He must be able to stretch his neck right out

red-letter day in the calendar of every hunt, for it is a
great social occasion. It also allows some return to be
made to the farmers for their hospitality during the
season, and it gives the more gallant sparks a chance to
try their hands at race-riding. By providing a delightful
day's entertainment for the casual visitor and producing a
gathering of the local hunting enthusiasts, it helps to
cement the good fellowship that hunting produces.

If you intend to point-to-point your horse as well as
genuinely hunting him, be sure that you buy an animal
that is of sufficient quality, probably a thoroughbred, and
has sufficient speed and intelligence to do both. There is
absolutely no reason why he should not do both, pro-

Whatever may be said of Aintree

vided he is a basically adaptable sort, and he is trained and ridden suitably. Naturally, his preparation for point-to-pointing will violate some of the principles on which his education as hunter has been based, for instead of approaching jumps steadily and tackling them circum-spectly he will be expected to gallop on and jump fluently without any hesitation or 'dwelling' at his fences. But a change of routine at the end of the hunting season should not affect his efficiency as a hunter, nor should it materially alter his performance in other competitive events, such as combined training, if his basic schooling is right. Indeed, for a horse as for a person, a change of employment and some excitement can be very refreshing.

Preparing a horse for point-to-point racing does not require continual galloping flat-out, nor should he be asked repeatedly to tackle big, formidable, fences at speed. It will not make him fit, indeed rather the reverse, and will only confuse him, leaving him wildly excitable or thoroughly soured. Plenty of steady exercise is required, for the horse should be fit and hard after the season's hunting, and a little sharpening up by a spin at top-speed over a kilometre or so three or four times a week should do this quite well. Getting him to jump fluently is also quite simple when you think it out, and will not be best achieved by galloping furiously round a circuit of enor-mous brush jumps. Much better to construct a number of small, solid, fences of faggots and rails, about three feet high, and after riding him round them at a sensible pace circle him into one of them without breaking his even canter, taking care that you 'go with him' as he leaps. Soon you will have him taking these fences in his stride without hesitation at take-off or landing. Take him at each fence separately, with the accent on calmness in between them, and you will soon have him jumping fluently. He already knows enough about jumping not to gallop into the bottom of a fence and he should be able to place himself, with only a little steadying or impulsion from you, to jump smoothly over anything that comes in his way.

He may need a slight change in diet if he is to work as fast as you intend, but this will involve little more than

Comparison of "forward" and "backward" positions

a small increase in the amount of carbohydrate you give him in the form of grain or high-energy cubes, and a little less hay. Don't stuff him with food, for it will only do him harm, and you may also make him ill. His intake of energy should more or less match his output when he is at work, and you need only feed him sufficient additional protein to support the day to day requirements of an energetic athlete, and these are not as great as many would have you believe. On the day of a race, about six hours should elapse between the morning feed and the race, and only a very small drink allowed about an hour before the start for, like you, he will probably be keyed up and have a dry mouth.

Always make a point of walking round the course you will later ride, carefully noting any variation of take-off and landing, fences at an awkward angle, drops, ditches and the differences in the going in various parts of the course. Get all these well into your head so that in the heat of the race you may still remember them. There will be places where you will need to ride gently, others where you can afford to press on. Note them carefully, for they may make all the difference between the winning and losing of a race. The rider must be as fit as the horse, in order to be able to give the help to the horse that he needs. Judgement of pace in its highest form is a magical gift, but a moderate capacity can be acquired by practice.

It is tremendously important, especially at the start of a race, to know at what speed you are progressing so as to avoid being hustled into a flat-out gallop over the first three fields, by a fellow-competitor who *may* be doing it on purpose to mislead you (a quite legitimate gambit) or, quite likely, is being run away with. If you keep up the requisite average those who have gone off so fast at the beginning will come back to you in time, having exhausted much of their horses' energies. Your every endeavour should be to ease your horse until you call on him for his final effort. Do not ride too short to be able to give your horse the use of your legs, but keep your weight constantly forward to free his loins. Keep contact, light but firm, with his mouth so that you can check any tendency to rolling or floundering by correcting his head

Pull him up and hack in

carriage and above all keep still in the saddle so that you do not provide extra stress.

Whatever may be said of Aintree (where the drops are colossal) it is perfectly possible to remain in the forward position throughout a point-to-point race and by doing so you will be saving and helping your horse to jump cleanly, fluently, and without a check at take-off or landing. He *must* be able to get his neck right out at his take-off and if you get 'left behind' this will be prevented by a jerk on his mouth just at the wrong moment which may even pull him down, as your weight on his loins may well make him drop his hind legs into the fence or a ditch on the far side. If the rider's feet are allowed to get the body forward of the knee the shock on landing may throw the body right into the air, and possibly off as well. At the best it will cause a check in the horse's recovery which may lose him two or three lengths over a jump. In a close finish the rider who keeps still, without disturbing the horse's balance and who therefore can give the horse the urge from the thighs and help him to keep balanced by a light pressure on the reins, combined with leg action, will beat the 'elbows and legs' merchant ninety-nine times out of a hundred, for the latter has lost contact with the horse's mouth, and flapping legs on the false ribs can only hinder him.

Remember that nearly all horses will strike off with their favourite leads, which they will change from fatigue after a short while. If it is a course with bends you may well find that you will be on the wrong leg at a crucial turn. Careful examination of the course beforehand may enable you to work it out and save yourself lengths at a critical point.

All horses like to race and enjoy galloping with the crowd, and there are very few who will not try to win. But if you see that your horse has had enough and cannot hope to win unless the leaders all drop dead, be sporting, pull him up, hack in and save him for another day. He has done his best for you and it is a scurvy requital to punish him for a gallant effort.

4

SHOWING AND DRESSAGE

The showground

The Show ring, from the largest of the national horse
shows to the most insignificant local country affair, is our
shop window in which are displayed the best examples of
our many, and still unequalled, breeds of horses and
ponies. The Hunters, the Cobs and Hacks, the Children's
Ponies and the Riding Horses; the great draught animals
of breeds such as the Shire, Clydesdale, Suffolk Punch
and Percheron; and the native and foreign breeds, shown
in hand or under saddle, which range from the aristocratic Arab to the ponies of Fell and Dale, the New
Forest, Dartmoor and Exmoor, Highland and Connemara,
Shetland and the several types of pony and cob from
Wales. And then in harness you will see the immaculately
turned out competitors for the Private Driving prizes,
from the simplest Governess Cart to the finest four-in-
hand of magnificent coach horses, all prepared and driven
by dedicated amateur 'whips'. In yet another section there
are the hackneys, shown in their special wagons and a
mass of fire and energy as they display their fascinatingly
unnatural action. The export value of well-bred animals
from Britain is considerable and the standard and interest
in pedigree horses has been maintained over the years so
that there is ample quality available to supply anyone
seeking foundation breeding stock, here or abroad.

Apart from the economic aspects, however, there is a
tremendous amount of fun to be had from showing your
horse, and opportunities for increasing his financial value

are also offered, for an outstanding show horse will command a very large price indeed, and even a moderately successful one a quite substantial amount. To combine business with pleasure is an enviable state, although it is highly unlikely that the beginner, however gifted with 'an eye for a horse' and experience in other branches of the equestrian game, will 'pick a winner' at the outset of a career in showing. The ropes have to be learned and the competition from professionals and dealers, who have spent their lives at the game, and from wealthy 'hobbyist' exhibitors, who can afford to go out and buy an animal that has already proved itself capable of carrying off a championship, is hard and remorseless, with a very high standard as a minimum. But it is a game which carries an enormous fascination for any horse-addict, although it is now a very specialised arm of equitation.

It nonetheless allows people to see that splendid animal at his most beautiful, and it also brings considerable trade to breeders and dealers in horses, and to the manufacturers and sellers of related 'horsey' commodities. It also provides varied and extremely enjoyable entertainment to hundreds of thousands of people who, if they may not be extremely knowledgeable, do still possess in great measure the traditional English love of the horse.

A wonderful choice lies at the disposal of the beginner who essays into showing. You may decide on breeding, in some ways the most fascinating aspect of all and with the possibility of rich rewards for success, but requiring considerable capital outlay. No breeding mare—from the toughest native ponies to the most elegant Arab—can be expected to thrive unless she is properly fed and housed and provided with plenty of top quality grazing. It may be more acceptable financially to go in for one of the various saddle classes—for Hunters, Hacks, Cobs, Riding Horses —with an animal that you have purchased, perhaps as an unschooled youngster, and 'brought on' yourself.

You may prefer to do the same thing in the breed classes, showing your pride either in hand or under saddle, or—if you have a suitable young enthusiast available— you could try getting up a Child's Pony for show. In yet another field of showing, and in some ways the most delightful for those to whom the competitive part of the business takes second place to the social side, there is Private Driving, a field where the most ordinary of animals can shine if his vehicle, harness and presentation are absolutely *right*. Here he can stand on equal terms with a horse which at other times may lead the hunting field, or beat all in combined training competitions. To be driven by his caring owner, as distinct from a stablehand in the style of the 1930s, will never harm a horse, whatever the traditionalists may tell you.

For the beginner, the chances are that the choice will be for a Hunter. This 'type' covers those animals which will do everything that a 'one-horse person' will require of them, hacking, hunting, hunter trailling, combined training, the occasional endurance ride, the odd turn in harness, the local riding club's dressage competition. He will also be a pleasant pet to have in the family. Hunters are shown in several classes, beginning with the 'Novice Hunters' who must have won fewer than a certain number of prizes and which may be of any height or weight. Since 'a good big 'un will always beat a good little 'un', the smaller animals are at something of a disadvantage in this group.

Then there are the 'Small Hunters', which must be below a certain height, usually fifteen hands two inches. Their 'weight', that is the weight they would be up to carrying in the hunting field, is not defined although it is implicitly accepted that they would be able to carry a light woman or man comfortably all day. Small Hunters, even if they are first-class animals in conformation and performance in the ring, would be too small to be considered in competition with 'Lightweight Hunters' which are generally expected to be up to seventy-six kilograms (which started life as twelve stones). The Lightweights are tall, usually a little over sixteen hands, and a little more 'leggy' than the Small Hunters.

The next group of Hunters are the 'Middleweights', up to weights from eighty-five kilograms (once thirteen and a half stones), to a maximum of ninety-five kilograms (fifteen stone). These are not thoroughbreds, as the Lightweight Hunters are, but usually TB crosses with a little more substance to give them the extra strength required. And there are the 'Heavyweight Hunters', well able to carry a man who weighs more than ninety-five kilograms (fifteen stones) and still show him the best of a day's sport. In all these Hunters the same basic attributes are required, the quality which will give the animal the fire and courage to tackle obstacles as he comes to them, a conformation which will enable him to carry his rider in comfort, and a degree of schooling which will make him a pleasure to ride. Hunters require a certain depth and reserve. They should give the impression that, if asked to do so, they would cover twelve miles of, say, the Heythrop's country at a workmanlike gallop without a single hesitation at any fence they met. Thus, when they are asked to gallop in the ring they should be ready to gallop *on* although they must give no suggestion of a desire to run away.

Show Hunters in the classes mentioned so far are not required to jump in the ring, but they would be expected to jump elegantly and cleanly in a class for 'Working Hunters'. In this group the way in which the animal performs over fences is taken into consideration as well as the way he 'goes' on the flat, and his conformation. 'Working Hunters' are not usually eligible for the most cherished of hunter prizes at any show, that of Champion Hunter. For this, the top two or three of each Show Hunter Class are considered on their merits, and the best of the bunch pulled out for the big prize.

The Show Hack is a very different animal from the Show Hunter, and, to some, more beautiful. The class evolved as one in which could be shown the animals ridden in the park, and they may still be imagined parading on Rotten Row on a sunny morning in days when everyone rode and the carriage was still the main means of local transport. At that time riding in the park was an occasion when the wealthy could meet and talk and, of course, the elegance of the turn-out and the quality of the horse was very important. Hacks do not, consequently, need the workmanlike qualities and reserves of speed and courage that are demanded of the hunter. Instead, they must be fine and light, with gaits which are almost dances and they should have a lightness to the hand and obedience

Showing Types

which make them pure delight to ride. These are horses which one would take out purely for pleasure, rather than as a means of being with hounds.

There are smaller ones, usually shown as 'Small Hacks', to a maximum of fifteen hands one inch, and 'Large Hacks', which are up to fifteen hands and three inches in height, and much lighter than Hunters, for their work is nothing like so demanding. They are often bred by some form of crossing of Arab and thoroughbred, with a little quality pony blood added somewhere along the line. When they perform in the ring they were not be expected to gallop, but instead must be able to execute an incredibly slow, smooth, collected canter and the most eye-catchingly showy of trots. They must also demonstrate their exquisite training in a brief individual 'show'.

Show Cobs are an interesting class, too, for their evolution is different yet again. Traditionally, the Cob was bred by crossing a draught horse with a thoroughbred, in the way that the 'Heavyweight Hunter' may be produced, and then crossing the result down to pony stock to reduce the size and introduce compactness and cleverness. The Cob was considered the mount of the elderly gentleman who did not require great speed of his horse, and did not want him to be too fiery, but did want an animal with obvious sense. The Cob must be up to considerable weight, and is judged as much for his abilities out hacking as his potential in the hunting field. He must have a basic quality, and no commonness, but is also expected to be very square in outline.

Until the docking of horses became illegal every cob was docked and hogged because it was felt that this increased the impression of squareness, but nowadays of course the tail is no more than 'pulled' at the top to make it narrow and the hair at the bottom cut a little shorter than that of other show animals would be. Yet another class of saddle horses are those shown as 'Riding Horses', which are not necessarily of the Hunter type nor are they educated to the level of the show Hack, but are judged purely on the basis of their appearance and performance as general purpose riding animals. This class may give the novice a very good introduction to the show ring, and leave a little more latitude than the more specific ones.

Showing is an expensive business if undertaken in a big way, for travelling, staying overnight and the hundred-and-one other necessities run away with money at an alarming rate. But the one-horse owner can have an immense amount of amusement by entering for the appropriate classes at local shows, and there are bound to be at least half a dozen within comfortable reach wherever you live, in the course of a season.

You may even try your luck at the County Show for, however unsuccessful you may be with your horse, it is a great thrill to be an exhibitor at one of these truly rural events where so many of the best products of the agricultural industry are on show.

The preparation for these shows will pleasantly fill all the spare time, and a good bit more, in the course of the show season, which is roughly from the beginning of May to the end of September. Provided, too, that your horse is not over-schooled to the point of sourness, nor overfed in the mistaken impression that 'high condition' to the point of fatness will enhance his looks, he should end a show season worth more, and far pleasanter to ride, than he was at the start of it.

Do not, however, expect too much or you will be certain of disappointment and it is a sound rule only to begin a showing career because you enjoy entering show classes, not because you like winning them. Certainly we all love to win, but if this is our only reason for taking a horse to a show we are depriving ourselves of much of the fun for, unless we are very brilliant or exceptionally lucky, we shall be disappointed many more times than not. But patient, hard work and storing up what you learn at every show—and there is *always* something to be learned whether you are exhibiting or just a spectator— will sooner or later bring you at least into the front row.

Judges are people of wide experience and of considerable attainments with the type of animal which they are judging, and most are remarkably free of prejudice and favour. If they were not it is unlikely that they would be judging, more than once, anyway. But they are bound to recognise certain horses, and also their riders if they have done well, however hard they may strive to be impartial. This is not entirely because some competitors are 'known', but because there is no doubt that a first-class rider in the ring and someone who is skilled at showing a horse to his best advantage will get much more out of a moderate horse than a moderate rider can get out of a really good one.

Remember, to, that while you have ridden only your own animal, the judges will have ridden all of them, and until you have actually ridden a horse your appreciation of him must be strictly limited.

'Ring-side judges' derive an immense amount of pleasure from their favourite pastime, in which they indulge to the full and this is the game of 'judge the judges'. No great harm is done as a rule, but perhaps it is as well not to be too outspoken in one's criticisms, at first anyway. It is, after all, reasonable to suppose that the most foolish of judges knows at least as much as we do ourselves about horses, and most have been at it for a good number of years. Also, they are in a position thoroughly to scrutinise each candidate, front, side, and rear. But there will be times when you find yourself very puzzled at a decision, although in most cases the explanation will be some minor defect which those on the rails could not have spotted, or else something only apparent on riding the horse.

Judging is a good spectator sport, and it is great fun to get your own catalogue and mark it with your own placings during the preliminary session, then compare your results with the official ones. This is a pleasure for all kinds of stock, and even the show vegetables, come to that (though how one cauliflower beats another I shall never know!), and at most of the agricultural shows there are judging classes for members of the Young Farmers' Club. It helps one to develop an 'eye' for a good animal (or vegetable), and is a good game. To reap full benefit from it, it is necessary to have a knowledgeable companion who can at least suggest some reasons for the final order. After a time, you will find that you are very seldom 'out' in the first three, and even the first half dozen places,

A bad ride for the judge

although the order itself may be a little different.

All this may seem to be a digression, but it is not, because this is the way to learn something of the standards and the tricks of the trade, and of acquiring something of the atmosphere of the show ring which you intend to grace in the future. A companion who is really knowledgeable and, preferably, also experienced as a judge or as a competitor is invaluable, for he or she will help you to form a picture of the kind of animal you require and of the combined appearance you hope to make with him. 'A little learning is a dangerous thing' and it is as well for the beginner to keep any ideas quiet. Very often they may be completely right, but it is desperately unwise to voice them unless you are quite sure that they will not be over-heard. Those who frequent the ring and go in for show-ing on a big scale have to put an enormous amount of hard work into it. They also put a lot of money into it. If they were not really keen they would not do so, for it is only a few who actually profit from it directly, and not many even indirectly, so far as getting their money back or making more is concerned. Accordingly you will find a good many of them a trifle 'touchy' and tact is essential, especially if you meet them just after a class in which they have been unsuccessful.

The ideal is to breed or acquire a youngster, break and school him and, at last, to carry off a Championship rosette. But the beginner, bearing in mind that it will probably be three or four seasons before he or she will be capable of winning in the ring even with an outstanding horse of championship class, will be well-advised, I think, to look about for a useful second-rater, past his first flush of youth and so possibly not too heavily priced. As in the case of hunting, we learn at least as much of the game from the horses we ride as we learn of ourselves. If a horse is also a useful hunter you have the use of him all the year round and the same should apply to a cob. A hack is a different thing, for he has to be taught or exer-cised in the performance of his manœuvres with the grace and precision of a dressage horse. Indeed, he may well attain quite a high level in dressage training too, for many of the basic training requirements are the same for both purposes.

Apart from acquiring a suitable animal for your needs and learning to ride him properly, it is important to develop 'the eye of the master' which can look at him, critically, as a whole. Indeed, this is essential whatever kind of horse you own, and your standard should always be the highest. To be sure, the best turned out horse in the world will not beat his betters but, on the other hand, a potential winner could well be deprived of victory by being badly turned out. When a horse comes into the ring he should have not a hair out of place, with a sheen on his coat that you can see your face in. If he is a Hunter, Hack, Cob, Riding Horse or Child's Pony, his mane should be neatly plaited into 'knobs'. His tail should be plaited if he is a Hack or a Child's Pony, and pulled so that it is narrow at the top and shows off his quarters to best advantage if he is a Hunter or Cob. For the breed classes, the usual requirement is a mane long and silky and tail combed out so that it is a glorious flag. But for each class there is a specific requirement as far as turn-out is concerned and you would be foolish to attempt to show your horse until you understood this thoroughly.

For most classes it is customary to oil the animal's hooves so that they shine, and for ridden animals there is the delightful custom of brushing squares on the horse's quarters. This was done originally by grooms who wanted to show that their charge's coat was really clean for it is achieved by brushing stripes in opposite directions so that the length of the hairs of the coat are visible at some points.

All saddlery must be polished and saddle-soaped until it shines, although you should remember not to put too much soap on the flaps and seat of the saddle, or the hand parts of the reins otherwise you, and the judge, will dismount a little grubby.

A showing bridle, which is usually a double bridle or has a pelham bit, is made with specially narrow straps, so that the horse's head is shown off, the noseband being particularly slim. The bit itself need not be vicious. Indeed, by implication, the shortest of 'Tom Thumb' curbs does your horse most credit and these are customary, with either a loose metal curb chain or a 'leather curb chain'.

If a horse requires a martingale or other gadget to keep him under control of course he has little chance of success in the show ring, and these are never used. The saddles used for showing are cut absolutely straight in the flap, so that the wearer's shoulder is shown off in all its beauty, and light leather girths are most often used. All the metalwork must be a winking dazzle, and the preparation of the saddlery is nothing more than a matter of practice and hard-work. And, naturally, you will see to it that your own appearance is immaculate for, if a dirty horse is a discredit to his rider, a slovenly turned out rider can equally discredit a horse.

Very delightful classes to watch are those for 'Ladies' mounts, Hunters, Hacks or Children's Ponies. These animals are shown under side-saddle, and the show ring is one of the few places where you will see horses and ponies ridden thus. Although in the hard practical world of to-day one would expect any rider, man or woman, to be equally capable of controlling any horse, these classes hark back to days when it would have been disgraceful for a woman to ride astride and, though she may have been as hard as nails underneath, the illusion of feminine weakness and helplessness had to be maintained.

In consequence the 'Ladies Hunter' must be of light-weight type—ladies are slim and delicate—but with perhaps a little more delicacy and grace and a little less of the workmanlike appearance of the ordinary 'Light-weight'.

The 'Ladies Hunter' must of course go beautifully under side-saddle and be perfectly obedient to his rider's every wish, even if the aids, which are given with only one leg against the horse are a trifle less definite. The evolution of the class also explains what is required of the 'Ladies Hack', the superb schooling, obedience and elegance of the ordinary hack, with that little bit of extra training that will ensure perfect behaviour under a side-saddle. The whole business of 'Ladies Hunters' and 'Ladies Hacks' is purely traditional, and in some ways illogical, since there are no classes for 'Gentlemen's Hunters'.

To see ourselves . . .
    'Wad but some Power the giftie gie us
    To see oursels as ithers see us.'

A horse which plays up in the ring stands a good chance of being sent out of it, for it would not be fair on the other competitors if he were allowed to continue and probably upset the others as well. Horses, being herd animals, love company and when they come among other horses are very likely to suffer from over-excitement.

Ride him about

Naturally a horse must be well fed and in tip-top condition but if he is not given sufficient exercise to work off any excess exuberance the result will be a form of intoxication that will render him extremely difficult to handle and will certainly cause him to lather and prance so that he does not appear at his best.

Nine-tenths of the input for a successful appearance in the ring is the protracted, patient, hard work at home. In other words, before a horse is shown it is essential that he should be schooled so well that his reactions to the aids are automatic, quiet and accurate, and that he should always be completely at the command of his rider. And this must apply even when other animals are playing up nearby, a brass band bursts into a military march just behind, him or a loudspeaker blares in his ear.

This cannot be achieved by long periods of intensive schooling just before the show, but has to be done by a gradual education in which short periods of 'lessons', at the most forty minutes at a single session and preferably only fifteen or twenty, are varied by plenty of interesting but steady hacking on the roads and tracks of your neighbourhood. Apart from the physical development and general well-being induced, this method is calculated to calm an excitable temperament and also to let the horse 'see the world'.

Steady exercise obviates 'over-freshness' and enhances *fitness*, which is quite a different thing. Think of the difference between the over-exuberant football spectator and the superbly fit player. You may also accustom your horse to unfamiliar noises by playing the radio in the stable when you are working on him, so that he will find nothing exceptionable in bands and loudspeakers. It is most important, too, to train your horse to go well 'in hand' and to make the most of himself for it is when their saddles are taken off the horses and they are trotted out and 'stood up' before the judges that decisions are made about conformation and natural action, which count for almost as much as the rest put together. When it comes to 'stripping' horses in the ring you will need an assistant to give you a hand and help give your animal that little extra polish, particularly under the saddle where he may be a trifle damp. He must look at his most handsome when he is called forward. It is usually a sound idea to give your horse a good hour's hacking and quiet riding before he enters the ring, with twenty minutes free to put a final polish on him and his tack before your class is due to be called. And do your very best to be on time, which will mean allowing spare time for the minor disasters which can happen to anyone.

When it is time to go into the ring, and especially if you are showing a young horse, it is best to enter behind a quiet, well-behaved, old stager, for if you follow another youngster which is excitable you may find that it is infectious. Remember, too, that your own horse will be certain to be aware of your own slight nervousness and will be affected by your feeling of tension. So many disappointed exhibitors leave the ring saying 'I simply can't understand my horse's playing up like that: he is always

Idle in the Ring

perfectly quiet at home and on the road'. Most must be unaware of the strange link between horse and rider whereby the horse is often aware of his rider's frame of mind before the rider is, which brings to mind a most remarkable sight on the opening day of the Royal Windsor Show a few years ago. This is the first, as it is the most enjoyable, of the major shows of the season. It was an Open Hack class and graced by practically every high-class hack in the country. So far from presenting a spectacle of deportment and grace, elegance and good manners, this class resolved itself practically into a *rodeo* exhibition. At one moment at least it appeared that there was not a single horse on an even keel and that a full half of them were on end. Not an atom of vice in the lot; nothing but high spirits and excitement, probably touched off by one young horse. But it was a memorable and a hilarious occasion and showed the danger of attempting to show a horse before he is ready for the ring. All of them could have done with another month's preparation, though no exhibitor wants to overdo it at the start of a season.

Naturally one wants to show one's horse to the best advantage and to make the best of his good points. A good 'front' invariably makes a good impression, particularly if it includes a 'good outlook'—an alert, interested expression of a horse who clearly has a good conceit of himself and is enjoying it all.

From the moment you enter the ring to the moment you leave it, you yourself must be 'at attention' and keep your horse interested, not only while the judges are looking at him, but also when, apparently, they are not—just in case. An occasional touch on the reins or a little squeeze of the legs, while standing in line awaiting your turn, will keep him awake. A horse, like a child, will get bored by standing still for a quarter of an hour, sometimes more, and he will either fidget or else relax into a sloppy position and show himself at his very worst. In the show ring you want to get the very best you can out of your horse and so must give him all the help you can. Here again it is a matter of legs all the time. Get well into your saddle, feet well back so that the aids can be given correctly, with as long a leather as you can comfortably manage.

Concentrate on your *own* horse: that is a full-time job for anyone, and do not allow your attention to be distracted by any attempt at conversation from your fellow-competitors. Be very careful to keep your place when circling round the ring. If horses are bunched the judges cannot see them properly and, sooner or later, the horses will begin to fret and 'play up'.

Never make an obvious attempt to catch the judge's eye. He will be looking out for you, never fear, but see to it that, at that moment, all is as it should be. If you have to 'argue' with your mount, try to select the moment when he is not looking at you. Be ready for the orders 'trot', 'canter', 'gallop', 'walk', in that order and get off on the right leg and promptly. If the horse is kept 'collected' he will strike off well enough.

Watch, too, that you are on the right leg at the canter and gallop and the right diagonal (sitting as the horse's inside foreleg hits the ground) at the trot, for otherwise the horse will be going false and not showing himself to the best advantage. Many exhibitors, some of them leading professionals, will keep their horses' heads bent away from the lead at the canter in an endeavour to improve the *coup d'œil* of their front to the judges and to keep

Don't race

them on the rails and into the corners. This is a false aid
and can be achieved better with the inner leg. Moreover
to bend the head away from the lead restricts the action
of the leading foreleg and shoulder and so the fluent
action that the horse should be showing. Remember, too,
that, though we talk of an 'off' or 'near' lead, this really
comes from a 'near' or 'off' hind support, obtained by
the pressure of the leg of the rider and not from the rein,
which is only a caution and a subsidiary aid.

One of the best ways of finding oneself in the back row
is by riding 'at' the judges. Judges are people of wide
experience and ability, otherwise they would not be judging, and they are perfectly capable of seeing for themselves, without a competitor shoving a horse under their
noses. They have the right to regard such behaviour as
impertinent. By all means take every fair advantage to
letting them obtain an unobstructed view of you and your
horse, but do not try to get out by yourself, by riding
inside the circle or by pressing forward or holding back
to get yourself into a gap. But watch for the chance of
placing yourself clearly in the judges' view and make sure
that, at that moment, your horse is doing himself full
justice. And when it comes to galloping in the Hunter
and cob classes for heaven's sake don't race. Children
are often the worst offenders in this respect.

Where the experienced professionals have an enormous advantage over the average amateur, and certainly over the beginner, is that they fully realise the importance of their horse's giving the judges a 'good ride'. Taking it by and large, the judges ride the exhibits 'according to the book', but a really astute expert, having discovered who is to judge the class concerned and knowing their personal idiosyncrasies, will prepare a horse to suit *them*. This is an art that cannot be taught and only long experience and the highest ability will bring it, but at least one can do one's best to ensure that one rides and applies the aids correctly. Therefore avoid any little tricks you may have discovered for yourself, or heard of, because the judge will certainly not perform them.

Regrettably, there is a certain amount of bad sportsmanship in the show ring, manifested for the most part in acid observations even in the ring itself and certainly outside it. Of course, as a condition of entry for most shows, the judge's decision must be accepted as final, and even to ask, purely for the sake of interest, why your horse was put down and another put up would be both rude and inconsiderate. The judges have worked hard with, as a rule, quite insufficient time at their disposal; they have ridden, perhaps, a couple of dozen horses of varying temperaments and eccentricities, and on coming out of the ring they yearn for peace, rest, and a large drink. It is unfair and unsporting to try to entrap them into justifying themselves: 'Don't shoot the pianist—he's doing his best.' In a similar manner, it is embarrassing for a judge when a competitor tries to ingratiate himself or herself, with a view to improving placings in subsequent show classes.

As in everything else, one does not begin to learn until one is actually doing the job. An ounce of practical experience is worth a ton of theory and it should be the object of the beginner to profit from each new appearance in the ring. If an experienced and knowledgeable friend is willing to watch your performances and subsequently criticise them you will find that this is most helpful, and you should endeavour to store up every detail for future reference and, sooner or later, the reward will come.

A final polish

Dressage

Dressage is, emphatically, practical equitation and any rider, of whatever experience, would be wise to acquire a basic understanding of its principles. In fact, it has relatively little to do with showing, having the same relationship with it as athletics to a beauty competition. In dressage, what is being judged is the degree to which horse and rider have become welded into one being, the horse's ability as an athlete and his control over his own movements, and his obedience to his rider's commands.

It is a fascinating and, at higher levels a most exacting, discipline in which a quite remarkable concordance can be achieved between horse and rider as they perform the more sophisticated movements of the advanced tests, such as piaffé, passage, and the dramatic turn on the haunches at a canter. And, rather beyond the abilities of most of us, there are also the 'airs above ground', such as the levade, courbette, and capriole, which are still to be seen performed by the magnificent Lipizzaner stallions at the Spanish Riding School in Vienna, a sight which is quite unforgettable.

But let us return to ground level, and the elementary and intermediate standards which are not so distant from most of us. The basis of dressage is that the horse should move fluently, with perfect balance and rhythm, and consistency, at whatever gait his rider desires. He must never fight or break this evenness, nor should he show any imbalance, such as a marked preference for one diagonal at the trot or one lead at the canter.

He must, of course, move quite straight when he is commanded to do so, with his spine in a straight line, but he must also be sufficiently flexible to bend his whole body in the correct direction when he is moving on a circle, either a full circle or the quarter circle which he must negotiate at each of the four corners of the arena.

Although the dressage tests are consistent, it is not permissible to train a horse in such a way that he could perform most of the test without any rider at all, as is indicated by his 'anticipating' movements. This would be directly opposing the objects of dressage training, which are that a horse should be entirely compliant with his rider's wishes. Dressage training begins with the correct and sympathetic breaking-in of the young animal. Unhurried training will allow him to develop mentally and physically so that he is never asked to do more than he is capable of and is not thus encouraged to develop bad habits as a means of meeting unreasonable demands. Training work on the lunge will help to develop the steady rhythm or *cadence* that is required, and the ability to bend his spine in the direction in which he is moving. Very careful bitting—with nothing more severe than a thick 'half moon' or jointed snaffle and perhaps a dropped noseband, correctly adjusted—and light, sensitive hands will gradually develop the correct head carriage, as he also acquires the ability to use his quarters to provide the necessary impulsion.

Dressage training is, above all, a type of equine education which cannot be hurried. It should continue throughout the life of any riding horse and though a short period in an arena marked out in the paddock or in a sand school may be ideal, much basic dressage training can be effected while you are hacking on the roads, which is quite frequently the only opportunity for schooling during the winter months when the ground is too wet for riding continually in one area of a field. Too often it is forgotten that dressage is the basis for *all* successful training and although the upper grades are very much a speciality, the elementary ones will benefit any horse and rider.

5

SHOW JUMPING
AND COMBINED TRAINING

Jumping in

Modern show jumping dates from about 1908, when the
Italian team trained by what were, then, revolutionary
methods and led by Captain Caprilli swept all before
them at England's greatest horse show at Olympia. It
took a long time for the value of the new style of riding
to sink in, in Europe as well as in Britain, but as it did
the standard of show jumping improved at an accelerating
rate. Over the forty years after the arrival of Caprilli's
methods, the British were very successful in the show
jumping area, the result of cumulative experience over
these years and the early adoption and teaching of a
'semi-Italianate' style of riding by the Army School of
Equitation at Weedon, which at that time had so much
say in equestrianism. The leadership of Lieutenant-
Colonel Mike Ansell, who was Chairman of the British
Show Jumping Association for so much of its development, must also be mentioned.

It is a natural tendency that each branch of equitation,
like any other form of sport or pastime, should become
more and more specialised as the quality of performance
improves in the light of experience. But, keeping pace
with it, there is always a steady improvement in the public
appreciation of the extraordinarily high standard of
general equitation demanded in these competitions. Indeed, in its early days show jumping was described as
'trick jumping' by riders who were ignorant of it, though

many of them were themselves fine performers in other fields. That type of comment died with the Second World War as it was realised that show jumping represents the accomplishment of one of the highest performances that a horse can achieve, with its variety of demands calling for the greatest possible fitness in man and horse, together with a flexibility that can only be developed by many hours of patient schooling on the ground.

But show jumping was to grow into a sport popular in many parts of the world, including Britain. It is a splendid spectator sport, combining as it does the excitement of the competition with the opportunity to watch the horse at his most athletic and beautiful, and the appearance of 'characters' among both horses and riders.

The coming of television, therefore, put show jumping among the front runners as far as public popularity is concerned, and ensured a large enough financial input from prizes, sponsored and unsponsored, and the buying and naming of horses by commercial firms for its growth to continue even faster than it was progressing before. The fences have grown, too, and those which are presented in quite ordinary events today would have looked like the dome of St. Paul's to the horses and riders of the earlier times. The standard of horse required has improved as well, as greater demands are made of him and the price which a potential show jumper will now call makes it well worth the breeders' while to go out of their way to produce suitable horses.

There has been increasing specialisation within the show jumping sphere as well as towards it. A horse particularly talented in speed events would never be asked to compete in any other type of competition, and the same applies to the puissance (or high jump) specialist, who will not have to worry about speed beyond keeping within a generous time allowance.

In most instances, however, a horse will be expected to be above all accurate, for to have a fence down will usually put him right out except in the final stages, and he must also be capable of a good turn of speed and the handiness which will allow him to take the short cuts that can save valuable tenths of seconds. At the top level

—and here we are considering the highest international grades and horses (and their riders) which spend their time on the international 'circuit'—the rider's part is enormously important, not only in the vital training and care of his 'string' but also in deciding on tactics in the arena. It is not purely a matter of chance that we see the same riders' names coming up again and again, and on many different horses over the years.

You do not have to be of international championship material to compete in show jumping competitions, however. At the lowest level there are the competitions at local horse shows, amateurish affairs and unaffiliated to the British Show Jumping Association, but enormous fun for everyone involved and demanding nothing more than a horse which will do as he is told without too much argument. Both prizes and fences are small, but these little shows do provide the novitiate, and particularly the one whose horse is also a novice, with an opportunity to 'have a go' without taking on the specialists and without having to find a horse that is worth a lot of money.

For most show jumping tyros the aim will be to compete, and perhaps succeed, in competitions at the slightly larger shows, many still on a local scale, but affiliated to the BSJA. Affiliation guarantees a certain minimum standard in the competitors, and of course it assures you that the fences and ground on which you will be performing will be of reasonable quality. The heights and spreads of the jumps are laid down in the BSJA's code, according to the grade of animals competing. In Grade C will be those horses whose winnings fall below a certain amount and these are the novices whose experience is limited but which are getting to know the ropes as far as show jumping goes. The entirely new entrants will be appearing in the Foxhunter classes, where the upper limit for winnings is lower than in Grade C, as are the fences.

The British Show Jumping Association maintains a record of the performances of horses registered with it, and horses may not compete at affiliated shows unless they are registered. This allows the Association to enforce its rules, for it has the power to punish a rider who breaks

Like the dome of St. Paul's

them by refusing to allow him or her to compete in competitions which are BSJA affiliated, and of course all of any importance are.

An example of how this power has been used to the benefit of show jumping horses is the banning of the practice of 'rapping', on the show ground at least. This technique consists of jumping a horse over a fence and suddenly raising a bar, of wood or iron, to give him a clout on the legs as he goes over, the object being to make him tuck his knees in and lift his quarters. Once this was a common sight at a show, but has not been seen for many years as a result of the BSJA's action. There can be no doubt that the Association's rule over the sport has been a firm but benevolent one, to the great advantage of all its participants, horses included.

What is the type of the ideal show jumper? This is perhaps the most difficult question of all to answer. During the very early days we are told that most of the horses seen jumping in the ring were hunters and, not surprisingly, for this employment they had their defects and virtues. To be sure, a jumper needs to be bold, fit and keen just like a hunter, but there the similarity ends. While a show jumper could be a good hunter, and occasionally an ex-jumper is seen in the hunting field, the converse is not true until the hunter has been practically taken to pieces and put together again.

There have been some outstanding show jumpers which have been very small in size, but as time goes on and the fences grow bigger we are seeing fewer horses under sixteen and a half hands come in to collect the prizes. This is not unreasonable, since an extra four or six inches in height gives a horse a considerable, automatic, advantage, provided that he is basically nimble and sufficiently well schooled to be able to perform at his best in the restricted space of a show jumping arena.

Many successful show jumpers have been only 'thoroughbred on one side of their heads' and there have been winners of all shapes and sizes. A mere glance will give you a good idea whether a horse will make a useful hunter—or at all events whether he won't—but many really great jumpers have notable defects of conformation.

'Italian' style as it was introduced

'Weedon' style owed much to the Italian

Some are rather common looking, some very aristocratic, others have been distinctly long in the back, and the only way one can find out is by trying them.

Some defects will always hinder a horse in the show jumping arena, a short neck being one of them for he needs to be able to use the weight of his head to the full as a balancer to help him to clear his fences. The saying 'no hock, no horse' is also true in most cases, as is Jorrocks' comment, 'It may be prejudice, but I confess I likes an 'oss's back wot inclines to a hog bend . . . rely upon it there's nothin' like the outward bow for makin' them date their leaps properly'. And Jorrocks was right, though probably for the wrong reasons. You will very seldom see a horse which jumps 'hollow backed' competing in top class events, and those odd horses that do must be quite exceptional athletes. The hollowing of the back is quite opposite to the stretching and rounding of the spine which is essential if an animal is to carry his own weight and that of his rider, together quite a considerable amount, over fences of five or six feet, or more.

In show jumping, balance is more important for horse and rider than in almost any other equestrian activity. The rider also needs to have a maximum of control and the position in the saddle must be absolutely secure. Modern show jumping saddles help in this respect, having a deep seat and high cantle, with flaps cut right forward almost onto the shoulder and with knee rolls. All these are designed to aid the rider in maintaining the correct, forward, almost folded, position which will give that power to the leg which is everything. The knees are pushed right *into* the saddle flap and the legs perhaps a trifle farther back than would be required for general purpose riding, to give that extra power and to compensate in some degree for the stirrup leather, which will be two or three holes shorter than would be used for hunting or combined training.

It is interesting, now that the Italianate system is absolutely universal, to look at its development in Britain. In the 1930s the 'Weedon' style of riding was considered very innovative and it, too, has contributed something to the method of riding we see in the show jumping ring

Flapping is not an aid

today. It differed from the more 'forward' styles, such as
the Italian, in that it insisted that the body of the rider
should be upright at all times other than during the leap
itself. This was alleged to enable the 'drive' to come from
the seat-bones and down the leg. The entirely Italian
system differed then in that the heel was drawn less far
back and pressed closer to the girth, with the rider's body
inclined forward at an angle of 45 degrees and the hands
low, well below the level of the withers, so that elbows
were bent at approximately 90 degrees, as shown in the
illustration. From a synthesis of these two styles evolved
the modern one, although we all owe much to the Italians
who introduced the new approach. A principle which
they explained all those years ago, and for which we
should be truly grateful, was that of correct positioning
of the hands. In order to avoid any interference with the
correct head carriage, which the horse has already been
taught, it is absolutely essential to keep the hands low.
Failing this there is a good chance that the horse's head

will be lifted just as he needs to stretch head and neck as far forward and downward as he can reach, thus breaking the fluency of his movement and inevitably disturbing his balance.

If you watch a really first-class show jumping rider in the ring, one of the first things you will notice is the stillness in the saddle, even as the horse twists and turns and leaps. The rider's legs hardly move at all. Compare this with what we see at less illustrious events where 'elbows an' legs, elbows an' legs' are all too common and are sometimes carried to the point of absurdity. 'Flapping' the legs is not a comprehensible aid to a horse; that comes from a squeeze, and in order to squeeze properly the leg must obviously remain in contact with the horse.

Many riders of the lower orders will also throw themselves forward, practically taking the air as the horse rises. To do so they must spring from their feet which means that, just as the horse needs stillness and urge from his rider, he is subjected to a downward and backward thrust as the rider becomes airborne. Another and important fault resulting from this strange trick is that contact between hand and mouth is lost completely. Those people who ride in this manner, often with the lower leg drawn back parallel with the ground and clear of the horse's back, show just how good their horses are, for they are performing at a great disadvantage compared with their better ridden competitors. Exaggeration is always undesirable and ineffective.

In the Italian position, which has the support of theory as well as practical success, the impression is one of a maximum of forward drive with the whole leg already in, and remaining in the ideal position to give the strongest urge and impulsion. The body being inclined forward at 45 degrees, the horse's neck is free so that all that is necessary is an extension of the arm to permit a horse to keep his mouth in a straight line with his shoulder, and at any rate the straight line between horse's bit and rider's elbow is always maintained.

Training jumpers
With regard to schooling a show jumper, and particu-

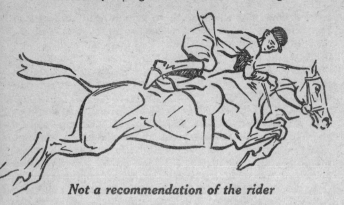

Not a recommendation of the rider

larly at the novice grades, there are two points to remember.

Firstly, the horse in the home paddock is a different creature from one introduced into the company of other horses, 'all fair rampin' with good livin' '. Just as in the case of a hunter going out to hunt being different from the same hunter which takes you out for a hack—the show jumper can easily forget much of his home-training in the excitement of the fray, unless it is so deeply inculcated that it is almost second nature to him. Also, most horses do naturally enjoy jumping as they enjoy, or can enjoy, anything they do, once they have been taught properly how to do it. And it is up to the rider to ensure that a horse continues to enjoy his jumping; not a difficult thing to achieve with the help of a little common sense.

How would you like to enter an athletic competition with a sore toe or a sprained tendon, or with your arms strapped to your sides, or with a pin in your shoe? If you ask a horse to jump with uncomfortable harness or when he is not entirely fit and sound you are asking him to do a very similar thing. It is surprising not that some animals become reluctant to jump, but that so many are willing to continue jumping. The last point in training for jumping, and it applies to all animal training, is that it can't be hurried and that the betting is heavily on you yourself being responsible for every mistake your horse may make.

A horse is not mature until he is six years old and the rider who is patient enough to wait for an animal to grow up before asking him to face large fences will ultimately reap the benefit in that the horse will have a much longer life and will perform better in the ring. We don't expect schoolchildren to be able to give of their best because they are neither mature (despite being fully grown) nor are they fully educated when they leave school; like your young horse, they still have much to learn of the ways of the world. In bringing on a young horse there is bound always to be some contest of wills between horse and rider and the latter must always win, but never through violence or ill-temper. Patience, firmness and kindness, allied to a full knowledge of the mechanics of jumping and riding, will always pull you through.

An invaluable and essential preparation for a show jumper is a reasonably high standard in basic dressage, with a particular emphasis on fluency and consistency of movement. These inevitably require that the animal is balanced with correct carriage and that he will be capable of a degree of collection, although this must not be over-done so that he can neither extend when required to do so, nor relax. The control, sympathy and synchronisation which dressage requires of the rider is what makes it so valuable, and is why ground work is so much more important in a show jumper's schooling than repeated jumping practice.

In show jumping as in any other branch of equestrian attainment, it is absolutely logical that dressage should be its basis, since dressage is, after all, aimed at perfection of the body's movements at the behest of the brain, in this instance the horse's movements and the rider's brain. The undisciplined and erratically developed body can have no chance against the trained one. What is more, the daily dressage work will also help to keep a horse fit, though the exercises will be for no more than twenty minutes, in just the same way as the ballet dancer keeps fit by daily 'practice at the bar'.

Horses may be seen competing in show jumping events

Cavaletti were introduced some time ago

in a weird variety of bridles, bits, gags, nose-bands and martingales. Some are very restrictive, such as the tight standing martingale. It is noticeable that this is seen less and less frequently as the fences become larger and the standard higher as you move up the grades.

The provision of patent bits, gags and the like all derive, presumably, from some defect in training, as an antidote to a fault. The horse has, to begin with at all events, a tender mouth. If this is considered and his early training not hurried and, above all, he is not subjected to pain in his mouth, either by a rough hand on the reins or the use of severe bits, he should remain tractable and responsive.

The thick, jointed, snaffle, either the cheeked, Fulmer, type or with eggbutt rings, is the most favoured bit still, although the gently curved but unjointed half moon, or even a rubber snaffle is probably preferable. A dropped noseband, properly adjusted to ensure that pressure is exerted on the corners of the horse's mouth—and *never* buckled tight with a view to preventing the unfortunate animal from opening his mouth—may be helpful. An alternative which is rarely seen but which can be of inestimable value in the training of any young horse, and indeed in riding any horse, is a simple cavesson-style noseband of the type used in a plain snaffle bridle, with rings sewn on either side so that reins may be attached to it. Thus the rider has two reins, a pair to the noseband and a pair to the bit, and will find that after a little schooling in this bridle the horse will respond almost as readily to a gentle pressure on the front of his nose as to one on his mouth. The noseband is not to be used to position the animal's head by brute strength, but it has an advantage. Once a horse has been taught to respond to it, he will suffer much less discomfort if an inexperienced rider (and that is all of us who have not reached Olympic standards) is caught off balance and cannot give him all the room he wants. (The idea behind the use of this device is not the same as that which underlies the use of the hackamore or bitless bridle on show jumpers whose mouths have been so badly damaged that they cannot stand having a bit in their mouths at all.)

In addition to his dressage training, the young show

When the demi-arrêt was new to England

jumper will benefit from work trotting over poles on the ground, which will—provided he is given the freedom to do it—make him stretch his head and neck forward and downward. Work over the cavaletti, which also came to England early on, will do the same and help both horse and rider to develop the muscles they need for jumping. This work will give the youngster confidence, and will help him to establish the rhythm which he requires if he is to maintain balance.

He will learn that, although he would, naturally, like to rush harum-scarum at these exciting jumps, he must approach them steadily but firmly and time each jump carefully rather than making a violent leap in the air and, in effect, shutting his eyes and hoping he has hurled himself clear of the fence. The great advantage of the cavaletti is that the horse is taught how to approach his fences without very much interference from his rider, and none of the horrible hauling and tugging that is sometimes seen. this, strangely, slows a horse down by destroying the fluency of his performance, so that when time is a deciding factor he is likely to do less well than the animal which has been trained to take his jumps calmly and steadily. A fit horse is bound to 'take hold' a little in the ring—it is all very exciting—and only long, patient, work will enable you to keep him in hand so that you can concentrate on the real business of the moment. This is obvious when you come to watch the international champions, who bring their horses into the ring keen but beautifully controlled considering how fit and of what 'high temperament' those animals are.

The over-excited horse which is fighting the bit from the beginning of his round to the end, and whose rider is continually wrestling to prevent him galloping furiously into his fences, is obviously at a disadvantage compared with the animal whose round is smooth and fluent. Each jump must be correctly timed, of course, and the horse's stride lengthened or shortened as he comes into the fence to ensure that he meets it exactly right.

For this, horse and rider must be in sufficient sympathy for the horse to respond to his rider's request to alter his stride so readily that to the watcher the change is almost undetectable. One technique for doing this is the *demi arrêt*, introduced many years ago by French and Italian jumpers, and usually delivered with one hand on the horse's neck and the other kept low.

Certainly, modern show jumping calls for exceptional control and the ability of a horse to vary his speed from the fastest to the slowest within a stride or two. It takes a long time and much hard work to develop. His handiness, too, must be outstanding if he is to turn into a large fence and in less than three strides alter his speed and stride so that he meets it perfectly.

Combined Training
Combined training is an equestrian sport which developed later than show jumping and in some respects is almost

So that he meets the fence perfectly

a child of it, though some experts would hotly deny that. Although riders show jump because they enjoy it, they also can expect to collect quite substantial prize money, if they are successful at the higher grades anyway. In combined training, the only reason for entering is because you enjoy it and—what is more—enjoy participating, with winning as a minor consideration.

Admittedly, the horse which has been successful in combined training events is worth a considerable sum of money but this is of secondary importance and combined training is, and we hope will continue to be, an essentially amateur sport. Because of this, its atmosphere is quite different from that of show jumping events, and there is very little overlap between them.

Combined training means simply that a horse has been taught to perform as he should in the dressage arena, that he has the courage, intelligence and athletic ability to deal successfully with a large, solid, course of cross-country obstacles as well as the handiness and skill to jump clear round a moderately large show jumping course.

Combined training may range from the three-day-event, such as the one held at Badminton and the Olympic competition, to the less taxing one-day-event in which local enthusiasts participate. The three-day-event consists of three phases, the first day's being the dressage test in which horse and rider must show that they have reached a standard where they can execute the basic gaits as required, collected or extended, with the horse's movements those of the supple, schooled, riding horse. They will also be required to perform some slightly more advanced exercises, such as the half-pass, in the test and in most contests the penalties scored during the dressage have a considerable bearing on the eventual placings.

On the second day is the 'Speed and Endurance' trial in which the horse is required to tackle five sections, all of which have very precise and taxing time limits. First will come the 'Roads and Tracks', a brisk hack over several miles, which is followed by the 'Steeplechase' section, a solo gallop round a full-sized steeplechase course of two or three miles. A few moments' rest to take breath and check that the horse is not being asked for more than

A course of natural solid fences

he can give, and on to the next section, another of 'Roads and Tracks', again to be completed within a set time limit. The fourth section is the most demanding, and certainly the most spectacular, for it is the cross-country one. A stiff course of large, solid, obstacles is presented which will test to the full a horse's and a rider's courage, and their ability to deal with large drops, jumps into lakes, fences round tight corners, high bullfinches, 'doubles' and 'trebles'—and almost any natural type of fence you care to think of. The section is tough, and penalties earned by falls or refusals or by running beyond the time allowed are vital to the final placings. The 'Speed and Endurance' trial is concluded with a gallop on the flat, usually for about one mile, to show that the horse, although he and his rider have probably had to draw heavily on their reserves to complete the rest of the trial, still have something in hand.

The test of Speed and Endurance demands that both horse and rider be very, very, fit, for its total distance will approach twenty miles. If a horse is not really fit he will be unable to tackle the third day's show jumping phase, in which he is asked to jump round a standard show jumping course. Although penalties for knocking down fences may not be enormous, they could still lose the competition and obviously a horse which is not fit enough to be able to come out supple and keen to do his best after the previous day's exertions will be at a great disadvantage.

The modern three-day-event represents the top grade of horse trials, and only the most bold and expert rider, and one with considerable experience and talent, is going to reach that standard. The smaller horse trials are, however, great fun and an excellent way in which to test your achievements in training your horse.

Not being on the scale of the three-day trial they do not make such demands on the horse, nor the rider, so that the amateur who has only a restricted amount of time available for training is able to enter with a sporting chance.

The one-day-event can provide an enormous amount of pleasure, as well as good companionship, and is based on the same three phases as the larger events, although they are usually presented in a different order with the dressage first, and at a rather less advanced level, followed by the show jumping test. The third phase is a cross-country trial rather than one of speed and endurance. It consists only of a course of natural, solid, fences which must be jumped without the horse or rider falling or refusing, and within a fixed time limit if you are to earn no penalties. The 'Roads and Tracks', 'Steeplechase', and gallop sections of the three-day-event's middle day are omitted.

It would, of course, be wrong to suggest that you will only find the able riders and horses in the two- and three-day trials, for some of the standards in the single-day events are very high. But they also include the classes in which the novice may 'have a go' and are the competitions in which the newcomer should make a first appearance. Combined training events also include some in which the cross-country jumping phase is omitted altogether, the tests being in dressage and show jumping and obviously these are much easier for the organisers to put on.

To whatever standard of combined training you may

The lower grades of show jumpers

essay, it is a most fascinating sport, the horse being trained as an 'all-rounder' with a basic schooling from which he can readily adapt to almost any other field of equestrianism. Although the really tough, top, horse trials are as much a specialisation as show jumping or showing are in their higher echelons, for the one-horse owner combined training at a local level is both very satisfying and readily attainable. Moreover, it will improve your horse's performance in any other task you set before him, whether hacking, hunting, showing, show jumping, or even private driving.

The type of horse required for combined training must, obviously, have considerable courage and speed, and he must also be 100 per cent sound. He should be quite intelligent. He must have adaptability as well as an agreeable disposition if he is to tackle the several phases with a cheerful enthusiasm. This must be tempered with calmness and steadiness bred by his good sense.

Most of these horses are thoroughbreds, though by no

means all. These are seldom thoroughbreds produced for racing and most will be descended from mares which have themselves done well and stallions whose progeny have proved themselves. Horses used for combined training are not always large and the smaller animal seems to be at no disadvantage, which is rather different from the current trend in show jumping.

One of combined training's main charms is that it provides no excuses for the illogical, unnecessary and often downright cruel methods of schooling which are sometimes used, and justified by their always having been used, in other riding events. Indeed, the schooling needed for combined training events is almost self-explanatory. It is a synthesis between what has already been described for hunting and show jumping, and—as has been suggested for these—a solid and continuing education in dressage. The benefit of dressage training is most evident if you watch the show jumping phase at some horse trials and then compare it with a show jumping event where the fences are of about the same size. The rounds at the horse trials are fluent and smooth, the horses do not fight and they are not laden with vicious bits and strapping, and yet they do not have any more fences down than the show jumpers which are supposed to be specialists in this field. And why? Because the combined training horse is assured of a proper basic schooling because this is essential if he is to attain a reasonable standard in the first phase of a horse trial. The show jumper, on the other hand, is frequently denied this, with the results all too obvious. There can be little doubt that, for many of us, to watch a horse performing at a combined training event is a real delight, while the sight of some of the lower grades of show jumpers in action makes one squirm.

6

SOME POINTS OF
STABLE MANAGEMENT

You may justifiably feel proud when you reach the stage where you can describe yourself as a 'horsemaster'. Until you can, however, you are not really fit to ride horses, and certainly should not own them. They are not the easiest of animals to look after and some of their needs are rather special compared with those of other animals people enjoy caring for. Although most horses are nowadays kept as pets, they are not nearly as well adapted to life close to man as are household animals like a dog or a cat.

Obedience
The large size of the horse can make him difficult to handle. It is therefore all the more essential that he be trained to obey the commands he is given, both in the stable and when he is being ridden, for if he once realises that he can do as he wishes this will soon become a habit. Fortunately horses are not particularly intelligent and are easily made fearful. This fear can be used, not cruelly but sufficiently to convince the animal that a certain mode of behaviour is not worthwhile. Thus, when a horse tries to barge through a gate and knock down the person leading him, a sharp word and jerk on the headrope will usually be enough to persuade him not to do it again.

Successful training on these lines depends on one proviso. This is basic to the training of all animals (and children for that matter!). The undesirable behaviour pattern, such as barging through doors and gates, must *always* meet with an unpleasant outcome, and preferably the same one. Moreover, the unpleasantness should come as *soon* after the naughty deed as possible.

For the most part, however, teaching a horse stable manners depends not on correction of naughtiness but on *reward* for the right response to a particular signal. For instance, a horse should allow you to pick up his hoof. When you run your hand down the lower part of his cannon bone and over the back of his fetlock he should take his weight off that foot and lift it for you. The 'reward' for this correct response is automatic to the horsemaster, who will speak kindly to the animal. *What* you say is not important—it may even be meaningless. It is the *tone of your voice*, which indicates your approval that matters. Unlike dogs, horses are not good at picking out individual words. They will master a few, such as 'Stand', 'Walk on', or 'Trot', but perhaps surprisingly are rarely clever enough to catch their own names. Sounds are much more important, and the clank of the lid of a feed bin, or the tone of a call to the gate for a meal, are readily learnt.

Because horses have a sense of hearing which is not good at distinguishing sounds in human language, the most useful means of communication is by touch. This is the basis of virtually all the 'aids' used in riding. It is also very important in handling horses in the stable. The way in which you touch a horse can make the difference between his being calm and confident when you are near him, or worried and fidgety, unsure where you are and what you will do next. Along with touch goes the way you move. Sudden movement is even more upsetting to a horse than it is to someone who is, for example, sitting in a dentist's chair. Steadiness and firmness are essential when you are with horses and in the stable it is vital that you move smoothly and purposefully, whatever you are doing. When you touch a horse, whether it is to pat him and stroke him for behaving well, or to groom him or put a bridle on him, do so firmly, so that he can feel exactly where your hand is. This does not mean that you have to exert great pressure, only that there is no hesitation. Once you have mastered how to touch a horse so that he likes the feel of your hand, it will help him if you touch him and speak to him each time you, for example, pass behind him or walk round him. This will let him know you are there. It is very important when you consider that the majority of kicks which people receive from horses are the consequence, not of the animal's viciousness, but of his natural response to seeing an unknown 'thing' moving behind him, which is to lash out with his only defence, his heels.

Watering and Feeding

There are many old tales about watering and feeding horses. Most are best forgotten for the animal's requirements are really quite simple. You should, first of all, ensure that he has clean, fresh, water always available and you let him drink whenever he wishes to. This is a safe policy, because most of the problems associated with horses becoming sick after drinking cold water arise because they have gulped down large amounts of water after long periods without a drink. This was a very common problem when horses were still used for transport and when mains water was often not on tap. Then, the amount of water offered to animals depended on how energetic the grooms were feeling.

The only problems likely to arise today are those of the horse which comes in exhausted and thirsty after, for example, a whole day's hunting without a drink. In this case it may help, particularly if the weather is cold and he is very tired, to give him his water warm rather than cold from the tap, and to allow a few minutes between each bucketful. And, as with yourself, you should always ensure that your horse's thirst is completely quenched before he begins to eat.

Various 'rules' are put forward for feeding horses, but you will not go far wrong if you remember that he is essentially a grazing animal. His digestive system is best adapted to a life of continual, steady, movement, grazing as he goes, so that his intake is in small amounts spread over most of the twenty-four hours. Admittedly, the horse does tend to graze more vigorously at certain times, when he is in effect taking a 'main meal', and much of the rest of the time is spent in picking, and he does rest too. But his way of life still differs very much from ours in that he does not naturally eat only three or four meals a day with nothing between them. We must bear this in mind when we try to keep a horse in the artificial environment of a stable.

The basis of the stabled horse's diet is hay. This—predictably—approaches grass more closely than other feeds, both in the nutrients it provides and because of the slow, thorough, chewing which it requires. This ensures that the horse must eat it slowly. Hay also provides horses with plenty of interest, for the grasses, clovers and weeds which it contains are all different and can be picked out, rather as one might select favourite vegetables from a stew.

The quality of hay is important and it should smell sweet and have no trace of mould in it as this indicates that it was damp when it was baled and subsequently over-heated. Horses seem to do best on fairly 'coarse' hays, that is, those which have been made when the grass is mature and has more stalk and seed heads than leaf. Such hay can be difficult to obtain, since it is not desirable for other types of livestock which do better on 'soft' hay. When only the latter is available it may be given to horses with some good quality straw to provide the extra fibre.

Besides hay, some sort of concentrate is also required for horses which are using a lot of energy, either in strenuous exercise or in keeping themselves warm in hard weather. The energy is supplied in corn, fed either as the grain itself or as a compounded feed which will come as 'nuts' or 'cubes' made from a mixture of ingredients such as crushed or ground grain, dried grass, molasses, edible oils, milling by-products and so on. The compounded horse foods are very good and of reliable quality which is very helpful, as is the ease with which they are fed. A problem with oats, which are the traditional grain for horses, is that they are best fed crushed, and if they are bought in this condition it is difficult to be sure of the quality of the grain (unless it is very bad). Also the oats deteriorate rapidly after crushing, losing much of their nutritional value within ten days or so. As the demand for bran decreases this is also becoming more difficult to obtain in reasonable quality, that is, sweet smelling and floury. Although it is useful to feed as a bran mash to tired animals it is again questionable whether the work entailed in feeding bran is justified when good compounded feeds are available which will supply all the nutrients required.

Shelter

It is now possible to buy pre-fabricated, rugged and surprisingly cheap stabling, provided that you have somewhere to put it up and a sound, hard base on which to stand it. Even if you lack either the place or the money required to equip your horse with such a luxury, it is remarkable what good accommodation can be found for horses if only their owners are willing to use a little ingenuity and effort. No equine, even the hardiest of ponies, will thrive as well without shelter as he will if he has a roof to keep the rain and snow off his back, a wall to act as a windbreak and a dry floor, bedded with straw, where he can lie down to rest. The animal which has to stand out in all weathers and has no 'dry lying' will cost more to feed, for he will need more energy to keep himself warm. He will be susceptible to disease, both minor things like cracked heels and mud fever, and more serious conditions.

Animals which have a fair proportion of native pony blood will do very well living outside throughout the year, provided they are given some shelter. This need be no more than a cart shed with two or three sides boarded up, but it will make a very big difference to the horses. They can be fed in such a building, which prevents wastage of the feed as it becomes soaked with rain. It is easy to 'deep litter' the floor so that there is always a thick layer of clean straw on top, even if the manure is allowed to build up underneath. It can then be cleaned out in summer, and you may even be lucky and find a keen gardener who will help with this job in exchange for the manure.

In summer all equines are plagued by flies, and the sight of horses standing head to tail, heads tossing and tails flicking, is a very typical one. Some daytime shelter will be welcomed if it produces shade and relief from the pestering insects. In summertime horses and ponies seem to adapt readily to a life of night-time eating and daytime standing, even when grass is their sole food.

In many respects, the easiest way to keep almost any horse is at grass all year, with a field shelter to keep off the weather, and whatever supplementary feeding you think necessary. He can be kept very fit in this way, for you can exercise him as much as you please. Because he has his freedom, you have the added advantage that if you cannot find the time to take him out for a hack he will be none the worse for it. This can be convenient if you have to pack many other things into a busy, modern, life. If the horse is to be hunted or worked hard in winter it may be necessary to clip him. If this is done only 'trace-high' he will be quite warm enough outside provided he is clothed with a well-fitting New Zealand rug and perhaps, in very hard weather, a night rug as well, underneath. Admittedly, horses which are kept out of doors cannot be groomed to the point of perfection that may be reached with the stabled animals which are clipped out. Nevertheless, the outdoor animals often seem to be sounder in the long run, and are less demanding of their owners' time.

A horse which is stabled all the time can look magnificent and perform like a ballet dancer, or, conversely, he can look very seedy and downtrodden. Even worse, he can turn into a raving lunatic if he is given too little exercise and interest and too much feed, particularly of the 'concentrate' type. Confined to a small box all the time, greater strains are placed on the animal's ability to adjust physically and mentally to the way of life.

The person caring for him must have a good knowledge of the horse's needs, so that they can be met as nearly as possible.

The first of these is interest and exercise, and a stabled horse needs about two hours of steady work a day, preferably through different areas and in new company, if his mind is to be kept anything approaching occupied. Interest is also provided by coming and going outside the stable, and for no reason whatever should the top halves of stable doors ever be closed. If the animal is so wild that he threatens to leap out it is not difficult to put a bar above the lower door, and if the horse is cold then he needs an extra blanket.

Grooming and other routine stable chores help to keep the animals occupied, as does the over-riding concern in any creature's mind, which is food. Plenty of hay and three or four small meals of oats or compound feed help to maintain a slow, steady flow of food. This is so important for horses in order both to prevent their developing the digestive upsets to which they are rather prone, and to ensure that they get the maximum nutritional value from the feed.

Health and sickness
Whether you own a horse or not, there is much to be learnt simply from watching the animals at every opportunity, for one of the most important things you will ever learn about them is the difference in their appearance in health and disease. The sooner you recognise that a horse is sick the sooner you will be able to do something about it, and in many instances this is crucial in deciding whether or not he will recover.

Nearly fifty years ago, a War Office publication described 'The Appearance of Health' in the horse thus:

'The forefeet are always square and firm on the ground, but one of the hind feet can be rested on the toe. It is noteworthy that the horse never rests a foreleg unless there is something the matter with it. The head is always alert, eyes wide open and ears pricking to and fro. The coat shines, and the skin may be rolled about on the muscles beneath, being loose and supple. The pulse is about 40; the breathing about 15 to the minute; the temperature 100; the colour of the lining of the eye and nostril is salmon pink. The bowels are moved frequently, on an average eight times in 24 hours, and the droppings are usually just soft enough to split as they fall on the ground. They should not be coated with slime, and their colour varies from golden yellow to dark green, according to the nature of the food. The urine is passed several times daily, in quantities of a quart or more, and is rather thick in appearance and light yellow in colour. Both horse and mare, when urinating, straddle, grunt and assume a very awkward position, with the skin of the quarters wrinkled, which should not be mistaken for pain.'

Much has changed since that description, for which I am grateful to the Ministry of Defence, was written in *Animal Management* 1933, but not the picture of a horse in good health.

The more you look at horses the more readily you will detect the signs of pain and fear which generally accompany their sickness. On the other hand, it is unwise to attempt to undertake your own diagnosis and treatment of animal disease unless you are sure it is of the mildest type and that, beneficial though your efforts are, they are necessary only to hasten a recovery which would have occurred anyway. If you are not certain of this it is wise to obtain veterinary advice early on in the course of events. This will not only save you a great deal of worry and your horse some discomfort. It may also make the difference between the horse's returning to soundness rapidly, rather than slowly or perhaps not at all. And it may also prevent your having to call out the unfortunate veterinarian at some ungodly hour, for as you watch them through the night a horse's symptoms can be relied upon to get steadily worse.

Some veterinary points for horse-owners
Colic. Horses are particularly sensitive to gut pain and discomfort is evinced by stamping, looking round to the flanks, kicking at his belly and trying to roll. If the animal is no more than restless the colic may pass off if he is walked for half an hour or so, but in most cases it is best to call the veterinary surgeon as soon as possible because colic, particularly if it is neglected, may have a fatal outcome.
Cracked heels and mud fever usually are associated with cold, wet, legs and they are sometimes encouraged by washing the animal's legs, particularly in cold weather. The conditions, which are essentially soreness and cracking of the skin of the lower leg, are best avoided by restricting attentions to simply brushing dry mud off the

legs with a dandy brush, and by providing the animal with somewhere dry to stand so that his legs will dry out. *Harness galls* do not occur on horses in the possession of a true 'horse-master'. They are the result of ill-fitting or poorly maintained harness which is hard and dirty and either so loose that it rocks about and rubs the horse's skin or so tight that it chafes. Every saddle room should be equipped with a leather punch to make extra holes in straps, and it is a sound rule that there should always be at least two holes to spare above and below a buckle. The most important treatment for all harness galls is removal of the cause of the trouble. If the sore is a serious one you may have to rest the horse from work for a week or two at least. All sorts of backwoods cures are suggested for harness sores, but none will work as well as this, painful though it may be to the would-be rider.

Laminitis is an exceedingly painful condition in which the fleshy 'leaves' inside the horse's feet become inflamed. The animal is evidently very reluctant to walk and the feet are very hot to the touch; in the interests of humanity the vet should be called as soon as practicable. The cause of laminitis remains a mystery although there is a fairly clear association with over-fatness in many cases, and once a horse or pony has had one attack of laminitis it seems that he is much more susceptible to subsequent ones.

Moulting occurs twice a year in horses, when they shed their heavy winter coats in the spring, in favour of the short summer fur, and when they shed their summer coats as the winter ones grow through in the autumn.

Over-reach, speedy cutting, forging. All these terms refer to a horse's damaging one limb with his other feet. When he over-reaches he cuts the heel of a front foot with the inside rim of a hind shoe; when he speedy cuts he gashes the inside of a fore-leg with the opposite shoe, and when he forges he bangs one hoof or shoe against another. All are controlled and reduced by good riding and ensuring that the animal is not asked to do more than he is fit for. A variety of boots and bandages may help to prevent physical damage.

Reproduction. A mare comes into season for about five

days in every three weeks and during this time she will accept the stallion. Mares first begin to come into season at about 18 months of age although it is not recommended that they be served until they are two or three years old. Most cease to come into season during the late autumn and winter, and also if they are being given very strenuous exercise. The gestation period of the mare is approximately 340 days. Most male horses are castrated (gelded) when they are about one year old because this makes them considerably easier to handle for general purposes.

Ringworm is a fungal skin infection which leads to characteristic, itchy, inflamed, disc-like areas of bald skin. In some instances it may be transmitted to people so that on the horse it should be treated promptly by the veterinary surgeon.

Shoeing. Costly but essential. Your horse's feet will require the attention of a registered shoeing smith at least once a month, even if it is only to pare the feet. The hooves, like your finger nails, grow continually and need to be trimmed to shape whether they are protected with shoes or not. Registration of farriers has reduced the amount of poor craftsmanship in this field, but it has also increased the price of a set of shoes.

Sprains of tendons and muscles. When these are mild, rest and hosing with cold water are simple remedies which will do no harm and—provided the horse is allowed to recover completely before going back to work—often work well. Where the injury is more serious, with considerable swelling, heat and pain, the veterinary surgeon is the one to deal with it.

Teeth. A horse's teeth are more important to him than many people realise and neglect of dentistry is a frequent cause of poor condition in older animals. Horses' big back teeth naturally wear at an angle which makes them less efficient as grinders and may even cut the animal's mouth. Regular inspection and filing, if necessary, is a routine job for the vet. When a horse's teeth are really giving him trouble you may notice his poor condition and a tendency to throw his feed around.

Thrush. A very smelly, purulent, discharge from the frog

of a horse's foot, the result of infection following his standing in wet manure and your failure to pick out the animal's feet which will help to keep them dry and clean. Removal of the cause of the trouble, cleaning out the feet thoroughly and smearing with 'stockholm tar' will usually settle mild cases, but where the trouble is more serious then the veterinarian should see it.

Vaccinations. Horses may be immunised against tetanus and this is well worth while, although it has to be kept up to date with periodic booster injections; the veterinary surgeon will tell you more about this. It is also possible to immunise horses against some of the influenza viruses which periodically devastate the horse world. It must be remembered that there are many different viruses involved and it is most unlikely that the same one will be responsible for consecutive epidemics of 'the cough'. Again, the vet will be able to help.

Worms are a problem which have to be dealt with by all horse-owners, and particularly those who have young animals and who keep large numbers of horses on small areas of pasture. The various types of worm inhabit horses' guts and the worm eggs are passed out with the animal's droppings, onto the pasture, and from there they are picked up by other grazing equines. Regular worming is therefore needed to keep down the number of worms in the animals, particularly when the horses have not reached maturity. It is also helpful if you can 'rest' the pasture by grazing other stock, such as cattle or sheep, on it for periods between chain-harrowing and rolling the grass.

Wounds and bruises are inevitable for any athlete, including the horse. When injuries are small, with little pain or swelling, they are best washed out with clean, lukewarm, water and patted dry with cotton wool or gauze fresh from its packet; some soothing ointment may also help to keep flies away in summer. If the animal is obviously uncomfortable, or the injury is painful, swollen or persistently bleeding then it is a job for the veterinary surgeon.

INDEX

155

SOME OF OUR OTHER BOOKS

Babies' Names A—Z

Buying or Selling a House

Right Way to Grow Fresh Vegetables

Handbook of Herbs

Right Way to Make Jams

Easymade Wine and Country Drinks

Pressure Cooking Properly Explained

Right Way to Keep Dogs

Car Driving in 2 Weeks

Highway Code Questions and Answers

Motoring Law A—Z

Game Fishing

Right Way to Speak in Public

Sample Social Speeches

The Exam Secret

These are Paperfronts, all uniform with this book

ELLIOT RIGHT WAY BOOKS, KINGSWOOD, SURREY

OUR PUBLISHING POLICY

HOW WE CHOOSE

Our policy is to consider every deserving manuscript and we can give special editorial help where an author is an authority on his subject but an inexperienced writer. We are rigorously selective in the choice of books we publish. We set the highest standards of editorial quality and accuracy. This means that a *Paperfront* is easy to understand and delightful to read. Where illustrations are necessary to convey points of detail, these are drawn up by a subject specialist artist from our panel.

HOW WE KEEP PRICES LOW

We aim for the big seller. This enables us to order enormous print runs and achieve the lowest price for you. Unfortunately, this means that you will not find in the *Paperfront* list any titles on obscure subjects of minority interest only. These could not be printed in large enough quantities to be sold for the low price at which we offer this series.

We sell almost all our *Paperfronts* at the same unit price. This saves a lot of fiddling about in our clerical departments and helps us to give you world-beating value. Under this system, the longer titles are offered at a price which we believe to be unmatched by any publisher in the world.

OUR DISTRIBUTION SYSTEM

Because of the competitive price, and the rapid turnover, *Paperfronts* are possibly the most profitable line a bookseller can handle. They are stocked by the best bookshops all over the world. It may be that your bookseller has run out of stock of a particular title. If so, he can order more from us at any time—we have a fine reputation for "same day" despatch, and we supply any order, however small (even a single copy), to any bookseller who has an account with us. We prefer you to buy from your bookseller, as this reminds him of the strong underlying public demand for *Paperfronts*. Members of the public who live in remote places, or who are housebound, or whose local bookseller is unco-operative, can order direct from us by post.

FREE

If you would like an up-to-date list of all paperfront titles currently available, send a stamped self-addressed envelope to
ELLIOT RIGHT WAY BOOKS, BRIGHTON RD.,
LOWER KINGSWOOD, SURREY, U.K.